P9-BJF-006

A CLASSIC RETELLING

The Adventures of

Tom Sawyer

by Mark Twain

nextext

Cover photograph: Dennis O'Clair/stone

Photo Research: Diane Hamilton

Printed in China

ISBN-13: 978-0-618-12053-6
ISBN-10: 0-618-12053-X

4 5 6 7 8 NPC 09 08 07 06

Table of Contents

Tom Sawyer, who lives with his Aunt Polly, is always in trouble. Aunt Polly says Tom skipped school for a swim. Tom runs out of the house and meets more trouble in the form of a new boy named Alfred Temple.

As punishment, Aunt Polly tells Tom that he has to spend the day painting the fence. Tom comes up with a great plan to get out of doing the work.

Chapter 14 102

Tom's Sneaky Visit Home

Tom worries that Aunt Polly is brokenhearted.
He sneaks back home to give her a note that
says he is safe.

Chapter 15 107

Storm in the Night

Back at the camp, Tom keeps his idea a secret.
The boys play for a while, and then Joe
announces that he's going home. Huck wants to
go, too. To stop them, Tom tells about his plan.

Chapter 16 112

Pirates at Their Own Funeral

Tom, Joe, and Huck watch their own funeral.

Chapter 17 115

Tom Reveals His Dream Secret

Tom explains the boys' adventure on Jackson's
Island and tells Aunt Polly that he dreamt of
her while he was away. Because he's now
"famous," Tom decides to play hard-to-get with
Becky. She comes up with her own plan to get
him back.

Vocabulary words appear in boldface type and are
footnoted. Specialized or technical words and phrases
appear in lightface type and are footnoted.

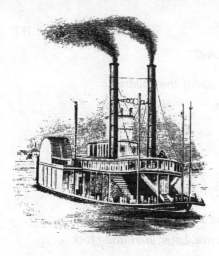

◀ A steamboat on the Mississippi River.

Background

The Mississippi River

The main waterway in the United States in the 1800s was the Mississippi River. The name, probably from the Chippewa language, means "large river." It runs for 2,348 miles, from upper Minnesota all the way down the middle of the country to Louisiana.

Ports were developed along the Mississippi River in the days of the pioneers. People and supplies moved along rivers on flatboats and rafts, stopping at ports along the way. In the 1830s, around the time *Tom Sawyer* is set, steamboats began moving up and down the river.

Setting in *Tom Sawyer*

Place

Tom Sawyer is set in the imaginary village of St. Petersburg, Missouri, on the banks of the Mississippi River. St. Petersburg is a tiny place where everyone knows everybody else. There are one church, one schoolhouse (which has only one room), and two taverns.

Some of the action of the story takes place on Cardiff Hill, a short hike from St. Petersburg. This is where the Widow Douglas lives. Another part of the story takes place on Jackson's Island. It lies in the Mississippi River, around three miles downstream from St. Petersburg. A small channel divides Jackson's Island from the Illinois shore. When Tom makes his secret trip home to see Polly, he first wades to the Illinois shore and then catches a ferryboat that goes back and forth between Illinois and Missouri.

Time

Twain says in a preface that *Tom Sawyer* takes place "thirty or forty years" before the time the book was written, in 1876. Twain himself lived in Hannibal, Missouri (the "real" St. Petersburg), from 1839 to 1853.

Characters in *Tom Sawyer*

Major Characters

There are many characters in *Tom Sawyer*. Here are some of the most important ones.

▲ Huck stared at the cross a while and then said with a shaky voice: "Tom, let's git out of here!"

Tom Sawyer—the hero. He acts badly sometimes but has a good heart. He loves to have fun and hates to work, so he turns almost any job he has into play.

Becky Thatcher—Tom's friend. She can be bad, but she too has a good heart. Unlike Tom, she is able to hide her weaknesses, so the adults all admire her.

Aunt Polly—Tom's aunt, who is raising him.

Huckleberry Finn—an "outcast" in St. Petersburg. He is dirty, lazy, and the son of the town drunk. All the children are fascinated by his "easy" life and long to be friends with him.

Injun Joe—the only truly evil character. He has murder in his heart and never forgets a thing. His desire for revenge leads him to kill Dr. Robinson and plan an attack on the Widow Douglas.

Minor Characters

Muff Potter—the town drunk who means well, but ends up in trouble because he can't keep his wits about him. He goes with Injun Joe to a grave-robbing and is later accused of murder.

Sid—Tom's half-brother. All the adults think that he is a "model child," but Sid likes to cause trouble in a sneaky way.

Mary—Aunt Polly's daughter. Mary is well-behaved and loving.

Widow Douglas—one of the richest people in town. The children all love her and want to visit her house.

Judge Thatcher—Becky's father. He searches for Tom and Becky when they become lost.

Mrs. Thatcher—Becky's mother. She is heartbroken when Becky is lost.

Dr. Robinson—a doctor who asks Injun Joe and Muff Potter to rob a grave for him.

Joe Harper—Tom's best friend. He joins Tom and Huck on their pirate adventure.

Sereny Harper—Joe's mother.

Mr. Walter—the Sunday-school superintendent.

Mr. Dobbins—the teacher.

Alfred Temple—a new boy in school.

Amy Lawrence—Tom's girl-friend before Becky.

the Spaniard—Injun Joe's partner in crime.

▲

"Thomas Sawyer, this is the most surprising confession I have ever heard. Take off your jacket at once." The teacher whacked Tom with the switch until his arm was sore.

Plot in *Tom Sawyer*

There are four story lines in *Tom Sawyer*. They are all connected in some way, but each story line works on its own. This graphic organizer shows the plot of each.

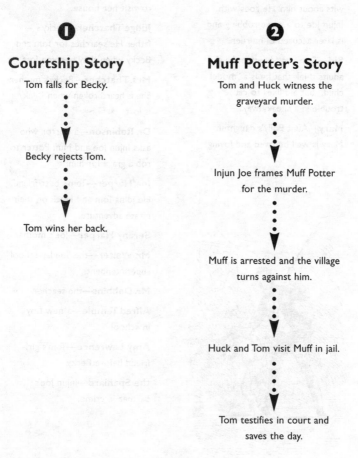

①

Courtship Story

Tom falls for Becky.

↓

Becky rejects Tom.

↓

Tom wins her back.

②

Muff Potter's Story

Tom and Huck witness the graveyard murder.

↓

Injun Joe frames Muff Potter for the murder.

↓

Muff is arrested and the village turns against him.

↓

Huck and Tom visit Muff in jail.

↓

Tom testifies in court and saves the day.

The candlelight disturbed the bats. They came flocking down by the hundreds, squeaking and darting at the candles. ▶

❸ Jackson's Island Story

Tom, Huck, and Joe run away to Jackson's Island.

The boys are pirates for a few days.

The boys return and watch their own funeral.

❹ Injun Joe and the Cave Story

Injun Joe flees the courtroom during Muff Potter's trial.

The boys discover him and the treasure at the haunted house.

The boys hunt for the treasure.

Tom and Becky are lost in the cave.

Tom sees the treasure and Injun Joe in the cave.

Injun Joe dies.

Tom and Huck get the treasure.

Themes in *Tom Sawyer*

There are many themes in *Tom Sawyer*. Here are some of the major ones.

A strong spirit will triumph.

Tom makes his own happiness. He believes in himself and never questions his abilities. When the other characters have doubts, Tom does his best to make them feel strong.

A child's world can be a dangerous place.

There are both fun and danger in Tom's life. All four story lines are about danger, fear, or death.

Revenge is a fact of life.

Injun Joe is motivated by revenge. But so is Tom. He's always looking for revenge on Sid and even runs away to "pay back" Becky and Aunt Polly.

Good wins over evil.

Because he is good, Tom is never hurt by Injun Joe. Injun Joe, on the other hand, dies a lonely, painful death because he is evil.

Dialect in *Tom Sawyer*

> "Hang the boy, cain't I never
> learn anything? Ain't he played me tricks
> enough for me t' know better?
> But old fools is the biggest
> fools there is. He 'pears t' know just
> how long he can tease a body before
> the anger starts . . ."

This is a classic example of Twain's use of dialect in *Tom Sawyer*. The term *dialect* refers to the way language is spoken by a particular group or in a particular area of the country. Distinct spellings, pronunciations, and ungrammatical expressions are sometimes used by writers to give the feel of dialect.

Spellings	t' know	to know
	'pears	appears
Pronunciations	cain't	can't
Ungrammatical expressions	can't I never learn anything?	can't I ever learn anything?
	old fools is the biggest fools	old fools are the biggest fools

Twain uses dialect to give you clues about the characters. His characters talk the way people on the Missouri frontier talked in the middle of the 1800s.

He also uses dialect to make you laugh. For example, Tom says things like "Consound it!" instead of "Confound it!" to express his disappointment.

Mark Twain (1835–1910)

Born in 1835 as Samuel Langhorne Clemens, Mark Twain was four years old when his family moved to Hannibal, Missouri. (The imaginary village of St. Petersburg, where *Tom Sawyer* is set, is very similar to the small town of Hannibal.)

At age thirteen, after his father died, Clemens began working in a local print shop. Ten years later, he took a job on a riverboat. He first traveled down the Mississippi River to New Orleans looking for adventure. During the Civil War, most boat travel up and down the river stopped. So in 1862 Clemens went west, again looking for adventure.

Clemens started writing around this time. But first he changed his name to "Mark Twain." The term *mark twain* comes from the language used on riverboats. It means that the water is deep enough for the boat to travel safely.

▲

The Author Engraving of the author.

Twain soon made a name for himself by publishing stories. In 1870, he married Olivia Langdon. (Many people say that Becky Thatcher is a young Olivia Langdon.) The same year, Twain began writing novels. *The Adventures of Tom Sawyer* was published in 1876. The book was not the success that Twain had hoped for. *The Adventures of Huckleberry Finn*, which is in many ways a continuation of *Tom Sawyer*, was published in 1884. This novel was very successful. *Tom Sawyer* and *Huckleberry Finn* are among Twain's greatest works.

As he grew older, Twain lost some of his light-heartedness. His stories and novels became a little darker, and the characters became a little meaner and a little less bright. This may be because Twain's later years were marked by tragedy. His beloved daughter, Susy, died in 1896. Olivia died in 1904, and another daughter died in 1909. Twain himself died of heart failure the following year.

Life of Mark Twain

1835—Samuel Langhorne Clemens is born in Florida, Missouri.

1839—Clemens's family moves to Hannibal, Missouri.

1857—Clemens travels the Mississippi River and becomes a riverboat captain.

1863—He first uses the pen name "Mark Twain."

1870—Twain marries Olivia Langdon.

1876—*The Adventures of Tom Sawyer* is published.

1884—*The Adventures of Huckleberry Finn* is published.

1910—Twain dies in Connecticut.

The Adventures of Tom Sawyer

CHAPTER ONE

Tom Plays, Fights, and Hides

Tom Sawyer, who lives with his Aunt Polly, is always in trouble. Aunt Polly says Tom skipped school for a swim. Tom runs out of the house and meets more trouble in the form of a new boy named Alfred Temple.

"TOM!"

No answer.

"Tom!"

No answer.

"What's wrong with that boy, I wonder?"

The old lady pulled her glasses down to the bottom of her nose and looked around the room.

"Y-o-u-u Tom!"

There was a slight noise behind her in the pantry.[1] She turned just in time to grab a small boy by the back of his pants.

"There you are! I should 'a thought of that pantry. What you been doing in there?"

"Nothing."

"Nothing! Look at your hands. And look at your mouth. What is that mess all over you?"

"I don't know, Aunt."

"Well, I know. It's jam—that's what it is. Forty times I've said if you didn't let that jam alone, I'd skin[2] you. Hand me that switch."[3] The switch was right behind him. The danger was close—

"A mouse! Look behind you, Aunt!"

The old lady whirled round and pulled her skirts out of danger. The moment her back was turned, Tom ran. He scrambled up a high fence and disappeared over the top.

His Aunt Polly stood surprised a moment, and then broke into a gentle laugh. "Hang[4] the boy, cain't I never learn anything? Ain't he played me tricks enough for me t' know better? But old fools is

---

[1] pantry—kitchen closet where food is kept.
[2] skin—punish.
[3] switch—tree branch used as a whip.
[4] Hang—darn.

the biggest fools there is. He 'pears[5] t' know just how long he can tease a body before the anger starts, and he knows that if he can make me laugh, it's all over and I can't hit him a lick."[6]

"But I worry about that child. I ain't[7] doing my duty by that boy,[8] and that's the Lord's truth, goodness knows. Spare the rod and spoil the child,[9] as the Good Book[10] says. But laws-a-me! He's my own dead sister's boy, poor thing, and I ain't got the heart to punish him, somehow. Well, I'll let him play hooky tonight. Then tomorrow, on Saturday, he'll have to work."

Tom did play hooky, and he had a very good time. He got back home barely in time to help Jim saw the wood for tomorrow's fire. Jim was Aunt Polly's slave. He chipped away at the wood, doing three-fourths the work, while Tom told stories about the day's adventures. Tom's half-brother Sid

"He knows that if he can make me laugh, it's all over and I can't hit him a lick."

---

[5] 'pears—appears.

[6] lick—bit.

[7] ain't—am not. *Ain't* is also used to mean "aren't," "hasn't," "haven't" and "isn't."

[8] doing my duty by that boy—Polly worries that she's not raising Tom to be a good boy.

[9] Spare the rod and spoil the child—proverb meaning that children sometimes need to be hit or they become bad.

[10] Good Book—Bible.

was already through with his part of the work. He was a quiet boy, and never had adventures as Tom did.

While Tom was eating his supper and stealing sugar whenever he could, Aunt Polly asked him questions about his day. She wanted to catch him in a lie. She said:

"Tom, it was awful warm in school today, warn't[11] it?"

"Yes'm."

"Powerful warm, warn't it?"

"Yes'm."

"Didn't you want to go in a-swimming, Tom?"

Tom felt a bit nervous, but there was no point in showing it. He searched Aunt Polly's face, but he couldn't tell what she was up to. So he said:

"No'm, I didn't want to swim. Not very much."

The old lady reached out her hand and felt Tom's shirt, and said: "But your shirt's a bit wet."

"Some of us dumped water on our heads at school. See?"

Aunt Polly was annoyed to think she hadn't thought of that possibility. "Bother! Well, go 'long

---

[11] warn't—wasn't.

with you. I'm sure you played hooky and went a-swimming. But I forgive ye, Tom. This time."

But Sid said: "Well, now, I think I did see him go swimming. I know I did."

"I should've known! Tom!" Aunt Polly yelled.

But Tom did not wait for the rest. As he went out at the door, he said: "Siddy, I'll lick[12] you for that."

---

[12] lick—beat.

CHAPTER TWO

The Glorious Whitewasher

As punishment, Aunt Polly tells Tom that he has to spend the day painting the fence. Tom comes up with a great plan to get out of doing the work.

Saturday morning was here, and all the summer world was bright and fresh. There was a song in every heart, cheer in every face, and a spring in every step.

Tom appeared on the sidewalk with a bucket of whitewash[1] and a long-handled brush. He looked at the fence he was supposed to paint, and all gladness left him. A deep sadness settled down upon his

---

[1] whitewash—white paint.

spirit. Thirty yards of fence, nine feet high. Life was all of a sudden very difficult.

Sighing, he dipped his brush and passed it along the upper plank of the fence. He repeated the steps one or two more times and then saw with disgust that it was going to take him the whole day to do the fence. Completely discouraged, he plopped down on a tree stump.

Suddenly, an idea came upon him. It was a great, magnificent idea!

He thought about all the fun he had planned for this day, and he felt worse and worse. Soon all the boys would come walking along on all sorts of wonderful **expeditions**,[2] and they would make fun of him for having to work on a Saturday. The thought of it burned him like fire. Suddenly, an idea came upon him. It was a great, magnificent idea! He took up his brush again and began whitewashing happily.

Presently, Ben Rogers came walking along. He was the boy whose teasing Tom had been dreading the most. As he drew near Tom, he slowed down a bit, but Tom paid no attention. He went on whitewashing. Ben stared a moment and then said:

---

[2] **expeditions**—adventures.

"Hello, old chap, you have to work, hey?"

Tom looked at the boy a bit, and then said, "What do you call work?"

"Why, ain't whitewashing work?"

Tom began whitewashing again, and answered carelessly: "Well, maybe it is, and maybe it ain't. All I know, is, it suits Tom Sawyer."

"Oh, come now, you don't mean you like it?"

The brush continued to move. "Like it?" Tom said. "Well, I don't see why I wouldn't like it. Does a boy get a chance to whitewash a fence every day?"

That put the thing in a new light. Ben stopped nibbling his apple. Tom swept his brush daintily back and forth—stepped back to look at his work—and then added another touch here and there. Ben watched every move and got more and more interested. Presently he said:

"Say, Tom, let me whitewash a little."

Tom thought about it, was about to say yes, but then he changed his mind. "No—no—I reckon[3] that won't work, Ben. You see, Aunt Polly's awful fussy about this fence. It's got to be done just right. I

---

[3] reckon—guess.

reckon there ain't one boy in a thousand that can do it the way it's got to be done."

"Is that so? Oh come, now—lemme[4] just try. I'd let you, if you was me, Tom," Ben pleaded.

"O, shucks, I'll be careful. Now lemme try. Say— I'll give you the core of my apple."

"Ben, I'd like to, honest I would. But Jim wanted to do it, and Aunt Polly wouldn't let him. Sid wanted to do it, and she wouldn't let him. Now don't you see the problem? If you was to start working on this fence and anything was to happen to it—"

"O, shucks, I'll be careful. Now lemme try. Say—I'll give you the core of my apple."

"No, Ben. I'm afraid—"

"I'll give you all of the apple!"

Tom gave up the brush with **reluctance**[5] in his face but happiness in his heart. And while Ben worked and sweated in the sun, Tom sat on a barrel in the shade close by and munched his apple. He sat and planned how he could trick more boys into painting.

[4] lemme—let me.
[5] **reluctance**—hesitation.

After awhile, there were plenty of boys, as he knew there would be. One boy after another came along to make fun, but then stayed to whitewash.

By the time Ben was tired out, Tom had traded the next chance to Billy Fisher for a kite. When Billy was done, Johnny Miller bought in for a dead rat and a string to swing it with. This went on, boy after boy, hour after hour.

When the fence was finally finished, Tom said to himself that it wasn't such a bad world, after all. With a smile on his face, he walked back into the house to tell Aunt Polly that the job was complete.

CHAPTER THREE

Busy at War and Love

With the fence completely painted, Tom is free to play. Later, he catches sight of a beautiful young girl with long, blond pigtails.

Tom presented himself before Aunt Polly, who was sitting by an open window in a pleasant room in the back of the house. This was Aunt Polly's bed-room, breakfast-room, dining room, and library combined.

"May I go and play now, Aunt?"

"What, already? How much have you done?"

"It's all done, Aunt."

"Tom, don't lie to me—I can't bear it."

"I ain't lying, Aunt, it is all done."

Aunt Polly didn't believe him, of course, so she went to check for herself. When she found the entire fence had been whitewashed, she was so astonished that she couldn't speak for a moment. Then she said:

"Well, I never! There's no getting round it, you can work when you have a mind to, Tom. Well, go 'long and play; but mind you get back sometime in a week, or I'll tan[1] you."

Then Tom skipped out and saw Sid standing just outside the door. Quick as a wink, he threw a dozen or more dirt balls at the boy before Aunt Polly could rush to the rescue. Before she could lay her hands on him, however, Tom was over the fence and gone. His soul was at peace again, now that he was even with Sid.

Tom raced around the block as fast as he could and headed toward the public square of the village. As he was passing by the house where Jeff Thatcher lived, he saw a new girl in the garden. She was a lovely little blue-eyed creature with yellow hair braided into two long tails. Tom fell in love with her immediately.

He stared at this angel with a secret eye until he saw that she had spotted him. Then he pretended like he hadn't seen her and began to show off in all

---

[1] tan—whip.

sorts of silly ways. He kept up this foolishness for some time, but eventually he saw that the little girl was moving back toward the house. Tom came up to the fence and leaned on it, **grieving,**[2] and hoping she would come back.

He moved closer and closer toward the pansy until his bare foot rested upon it.

She halted a moment on the steps and then moved toward the door. Tom let out a great sigh as she put her hand on the knob. Before she walked into the house, however, she tossed a pansy[3] over the fence at Tom.

Tom ran around and stopped within a foot or two of the flower. Then he shaded his eyes with his hand and began to look up and down the street to be sure no one was watching. He moved closer and closer toward the pansy until his bare foot rested upon it. With a quick movement, his toes closed upon it, and he hopped away home with the treasure between his toes and his head full of thoughts of the girl.

All through supper Tom's spirits were so high that his aunt wondered "what had got into the child." She yelled at him for throwing dirt at Sid,

---

[2] **grieving**—feeling sad because someone is gone or dead.
[3] pansy—small flower similar to a violet.

but he did not seem to mind it in the least. He tried to steal sugar under his aunt's very nose, and got his knuckles smacked for it. He said: "Aunt, you don't whack Sid when he takes it."

"Well, Sid don't tease the way you do. You'd always be into that sugar if I warn't watching you."

Presently she stepped into the kitchen, and Sid happily reached for the sugar bowl. But Sid's fingers slipped and the bowl dropped and broke. Tom was thrilled. There would be nothing so good in the world as to see Sid the Perfect get into trouble!

When Aunt Polly came back and stood above the broken sugar bowl, he said to himself, "Now it's coming!" And the next instant he was sprawling on the floor! Aunt Polly's palm was raised to strike again when Tom cried out:

"Hold on, now, what are you hitting me for?—Sid broke it!"

Aunt Polly paused and thought for a moment. Then she said: "Umf! Well you deserved that for something else that I don't know about, I'm sure."

But then Polly felt terrible, and wanted to say a loving word to the boy. She stopped herself, though, because she knew that she couldn't admit that she had been in the wrong. She'd never get him to mind her again. So she kept silent, but her heart was troubled.

Tom **sulked**[4] in a corner. He was so busy feeling sorry for himself that he didn't even notice when his cousin Mary danced in, all happy from her week-long visit to the country. He moved out the door without saying even a word of hello. Feeling low and unhappy, he wandered down to the river. He sat on the edge of a log raft and wished that he could drown without feeling any kind of pain or **discomfort**.[5] At last he got up, sighing, and made his way home. He crept into the house and upstairs to his room.

Sid woke up when Tom came in, although he didn't dare say a word. He saw that Tom had danger his eye. Tom jumped into bed without bothering to say his prayers, and Sid made sure he'd remember the **omission**.[6]

---

[4] **sulked**—pouted.

[5] **discomfort**—distress, suffering, or grief.

[6] **omission**—oversight; something not done.

CHAPTER FOUR

Showing Off in Sunday-School

Tom trades a collection of his "treasures" for a stack of Sunday-school tickets. Judge Thatcher, Mrs. Thatcher, and Becky visit the Sunday-school. The Thatchers think Tom is a great student until they find that he can't answer even the simplest question about what he's learned.

Sunday was just as lovely as Saturday. As soon as breakfast was over, Aunt Polly led the family in prayer. Then Tom went to work hard at learning his five verses.[1] He chose the shortest ones he could. At the end of a half an hour, he had a vague idea of what his Sunday-school lesson was to be. Mary

---

[1] verses—passages from the Bible.

took his book to hear him **recite**,[2] and he tried to find his way through the fog:

"Blessed are the—a—a—"

"Poor—"

"Yes—poor; blessed are the poor—a—a—"

"In spirit—"

"In spirit; blessed are the poor in spirit, for they—they—"

"Theirs—"

"For theirs. Blessed are the poor in spirit, for theirs is the kingdom of heaven. Blessed are they that mourn, for they—they—"[3]

"Shall!" Mary **prompted**,[4] a little bit annoyed.

"OK, *shall!* Oh, why don't you just tell me, Mary? What do you want to be so mean for?"

"Oh, Tom, you poor thick-headed thing, I'm not being mean. You have to learn it. Don't give up, Tom, you'll memorize it in the end. And if you do, I'll give you something ever so nice."

So Tom went back over his lessons again. Finally, he learned the whole thing, and Mary gave him a brand-new pocket knife worth twelve-and-a-half cents. He shivered with pleasure and immediately went to work carving the top of his dresser. Mary

---

[2] **recite**—say something aloud from memory.

[3] Blessed are the . . ."—Tom is trying to recite verses from Jesus's Sermon on the Mount (Matthew 5:7).

[4] **prompted**—helped him by saying the next word.

put a stop to that as soon as she noticed, but not before Tom had made some really good scratches.

Soon enough, the three children set out for Sunday-school—a place that Tom hated with his whole heart. Unfortunately, Sid and Mary were fond of it.

Sunday-school hours were from nine to eleven, with a church service afterward. As they walked toward the church, Tom shouted back and forth with his friends. On his way into the church, Tom dropped back and whispered to another boy:

"Say, Billy, got a yellow ticket?"

"Yes. What'll you give me for it?"

"Say, Billy, got a yellow ticket?"

"Yes. What'll you give me for it?"

"Piece of candy and a fish-hook," Tom replied.

With a nod, Billy handed over his yellow ticket and Tom thrust it into his pocket. Then Tom traded a couple of marbles for some blue tickets and went on trading whatever he had in his pockets for tickets of different colors. Soon he had traded away everything he had earned on Saturday during the whitewashing. For his effort, he had a neat little stack of tickets.

When the boys reached the classroom, the teacher put a stop to the trades and had the children come up one by one to recite their verses. None of them knew his verses very well, but the teacher was willing to help. Afterward, each child got a blue ticket for every two verses he or she had learned. In time, they could cash in ten of their blue tickets for a red ticket. After that, they could cash in ten red tickets for a yellow ticket, which was the most valuable kind of ticket. For ten yellow tickets, the **Superintendent**[5] of the Sunday-school gave a very plain Bible (worth forty cents in those easy times). Mary had earned two Bibles because she was so good, but it took most children years and years to earn enough tickets.

Since it was so rare for a child to earn a Bible, the Superintendent and the teachers made a very big fuss on the day a Bible was to be presented. Although Tom wasn't really interested in a Bible, he *was* interested in having everyone make a fuss over him. So, like the other children in the school, Tom saved his tickets like mad.

At last the Superintendent stood up in front of the **pulpit**,[6] with a closed hymn-book in his hand and asked for "silence!" Then he began speaking in his best Sunday-school Superintendent voice:

---

[5] **Superintendent**—director.

[6] **pulpit**—platform from which a minister speaks.

"Now children, I want you all to sit up just as straight and pretty as you can and give me all your attention for a minute or two. I want to tell you how good it makes me feel to see so many bright, clean little faces all in one place like this, where you'll learn to do right and be good."

The whole class looked up happily when the man was finally silent.

Mr. Waters went on like this for quite some time, and Tom stopped listening. He heard the same kind of speech every Sunday.

During the final half of the speech, there was some whispering and poking among a few of the bad boys. But every sound stopped as soon as Mr. Walters stopped talking. The whole class looked up happily when the man was finally silent.

Most of the whispering had been about a visitor to the classroom—the lawyer Thatcher, who was accompanied by a fine, portly,[7] middle-aged gentleman with iron-gray hair and a **dignified**[8] lady who was clearly the portly man's wife. The lady was leading a child. Tom had been restless while the superintendent was speaking, but when he saw the small newcomer, his heart leapt for joy. It was the girl with the pansy!

---

[7] portly—fat.
[8] **dignified**—elegant; important-looking.

The visitors were given the highest seat of honor. As soon as Mr. Walters's speech was finished, he introduced them to the school. The middle-aged man turned out to be an important county judge. He was from Constantinople, which was twelve miles away. So this man had traveled! He had seen the world! Tom studied him with respect. This was the great Judge Thatcher, brother of their own lawyer Thatcher.

Mr. Walters was simply thrilled to have such an important person visiting his Sunday school. If only there was a chance to deliver a Bible-prize today! He'd give anything to be able to show off one of his pupils in front of the judge. But he had checked carefully. Several pupils had a few yellow tickets, but none had enough.

And yet at this moment, when all hope was dead, Tom Sawyer came forward with nine yellow tickets, nine red tickets, and ten blue ones, and demanded a Bible. This was simply amazing! Walters had thought that it would take Tom ten more years to earn a Bible. But there was no getting around it—here were the exact number of tickets needed.

It was the most stunning surprise in years. All the boys were eaten up with envy. The most jealous boys were the boys who realized they had helped Tom gather enough tickets by trading theirs away.

All of a sudden, these boys **despised**[9] themselves, and knew that they had been tricked by a **wily**[10] boy named Tom Sawyer.

The prize was delivered to Tom with as much fuss as the Superintendent could pump up at such short notice. Tom's girlfriend Amy Lawrence was proud and glad, and she tried to make Tom see it in her face—but he wouldn't look at her. She wondered about this and then realized the truth when she saw the sneaky little glances the boy was giving to the Thatcher girl. Amy was jealous and angry, and the tears came, and she hated everybody—Tom most of all.

Tom was introduced to the judge, but his tongue was tied and he couldn't say a word. The judge put his hand on Tom's head and called him a fine little man, and asked him what his name was. The boy stammered, gasped, and got it out:

"Tom Sawyer."

"That's it! That's a good boy," the great judge replied. "Two thousand verses is a great many—a very, very great many. And you'll never be sorry for the trouble you took to learn them, for knowledge

---

[9] **despised**—hated.
[10] **wily**—clever.

is worth more than anything in the world. Now, would you be so good as to tell me and this lady some of the things you've learned? No doubt you know the names of all the twelve Disciples.[11] Won't you tell us the names of the first two?"

Tom was tugging at a button and looking shy.

Tom was tugging at a button and looking shy. He blushed, now, and his eyes fell. Mr. Walters's heart sank within him. He said to himself, "The boy will never be able to answer. Oh, why did the judge have to ask him a question?" Yet he felt he must speak up and said:

"Answer the judge, Tom—don't be afraid."

Tom still hung his head down.

"Now I know you'll tell me" said the lady. "The names of the first two disciples were—"

"DAVID AND GOLIATH!"[12] Tom blurted in a voice loud enough for the whole church to hear.

With this answer, we'll draw a curtain over this most awful scene.

---

[11] Disciples—twelve men who followed Jesus and preached his messages.

[12] DAVID AND GOLIATH—In the Bible, David was a king of the ancient Hebrews, who as a boy killed a giant named Goliath. Tom was supposed to answer, "Peter and Andrew."

CHAPTER FIVE

Tom Meets Becky

On his way to school, Tom runs into Huckleberry Finn. Huck is the son of a drunk and the opposite of a "model boy." Tom and Huck make a plan to visit the cemetery around midnight. At school, Tom meets Becky for the first time.

On Monday morning, Tom Sawyer was miserable. In fact, he was miserable every Monday morning, because it meant another week's slow suffering in school.

Tom lay thinking. He wondered if he might be sick, which would allow him to stay home from school. Slowly, he checked his system. He didn't feel sick, but he wasn't ready to give up yet. Eventually, he remembered that one of his upper front teeth was loose. He was about to call for his aunt, but realized that she would merely pull it out.

So that was no good. Then he thought about his toe, and decided that it was still quite sore. He started moaning and groaning in an attempt to wake up Sid.

On and on he groaned, but Sid did not stir. Finally, he became annoyed. He said, "Sid, Sid!" and shook him a bit. Then he fell back into his bed and started groaning again.

"Oh, Tom, you ain't dying, are you?"

Sid said: "Tom! Say, Tom!" [No response.] "Here, Tom! Tom! What is the matter, Tom?" Then he started to shake him and looked at Tom's face anxiously.

Tom moaned out: "Oh don't, Sid. Don't joggle me."

"But what's the matter, Tom? I must call Auntie."

"No—never mind. It'll be over soon, I think. Don't call anybody."

"But I must! Don't moan so, Tom, it's awful. How long have you been in pain?"

"Hours."

"Tom, why didn't you wake me sooner? Oh, Tom, you ain't dying, are you? Don't die, Tom—Oh, don't—"

Without finishing, Sid snatched his clothes and flew down the stairs, yelling all the way: "Oh, Aunt Polly, come! Tom's dying!"

"Dying!"

"Yes'm. Don't wait—come quick!"

"Garbage! I don't believe it!" But she fled up the stairs with Sid and Mary at her heels. And her face grew white, too, and her lip trembled. When she reached the bedside, she gasped out:

"You Tom! Tom, what's the matter with you?"

"Oh, Auntie, I'm—"

"What's the matter with you—what is the matter with you, child!"

"Oh, Auntie, my sore toe—it's killing me!"

The old lady sank down into a chair and laughed a little, then cried a little, then did both together. Then she said: "Oh, Tom, you scared me to death. Now you shut up that nonsense and get dressed for school."

Tom stopped groaning and the pain vanished from his toe. He felt a little foolish, so he did what he was supposed to do and made his way down for breakfast. Before he left, however, his aunt insisted on pulling the tooth that was "aching" so badly.

As he walked to school, Tom realized that he was the envy of all his friends because of the gap in the upper row of his teeth. He could now spit in a new and interesting way. Tom enjoyed his new trick all the way through the village square. There he met the worst boy in all the village, Huckleberry Finn, who was the son of the town drunkard.[1]

> *Huckleberry was hated by all the mothers of the town because he was lazy and lawless and vulgar and bad.*

Huckleberry was hated by all the mothers of the town because he was lazy and lawless and **vulgar**[2] and bad. Plus, all the children admired him so much, and this made the mothers feel nervous. Tom was like all the other boys. He admired Huck and was jealous of the fact that he was such an **outcast**.[3]

Of course, Aunt Polly had told Tom never to play with Huck. But Tom played with him every chance he could. Today, Huck was dressed in his usual assortment of hand-me-down clothes and rags.

What fascinated Tom the most was that Huckleberry came and went at his own free will. He slept on doorsteps in fine weather and in empty barns when it rained. He did not have to go to school or church and did not have to mind his manners.

---

[1] drunkard—person who drinks too much alcohol.

[2] **vulgar**—rude and crude; disgusting.

[3] **outcast**—person who is looked down on by others.

He was always the first boy to go barefoot in the spring and the last to put on shoes in the fall. He never had to wash or put on clean clothes. Huck's life was perfect.

Tom called to the boy. "Hello, Huckleberry!"

"Hello yourself, Tom Sawyer."

"What's that you have in your hand, Huck?"

"It's a dead cat."

"Lemme see him, Huck. My, he's pretty stiff. What's he good for?"

"I'm gonna cure warts with him."

"No! Is that so?"

"Cert'nly," Huck replied. "I'll tell you how it's done. You take your cat and go to the graveyard at around midnight. You go to where someone wicked has been buried. At midnight, when the devils come, you throw your cat at the gravestone and say 'Devil follow **corpse**,[4] cat follow devil, warts follow cat, I'm done with ye!' That'll fix any wart."

"Sounds right. Did you ever try it, Huck?"

"No, but old Mother Hopkins told me about it."

"Well I reckon it's true then, becuz she's a witch."

"Ain't that the truth. She witched my pap.[5] He says so hisself. He was walking along one day and she put a spell on him. That very night, he rolled off

---

[4] **corpse**—dead body.

[5] pap—Huck calls his father "Pap."

a roof where he was sleeping becuz he was drunk. He broke his arm."

"Why that's awful." Tom paused to think things over. "Say, Huck, when you going to try the cat?"

"Tonight. I'm a-going to try my luck at old Hoss Williams's grave, since he just died and he was nasty enough."

"Will you lemme go with you?" Tom pleaded.

"Of course—if you ain't afraid."

"Afraid! That ain't likely," Tom replied.

"All right, Tom. I'll meow for you when it's time."

Right before he walked away, he pulled out a tick[6] and showed it to Tom. Tom was fascinated by the little bug and told Huck he'd trade him his tooth for it. Huck thought about it for awhile and then realized it was a fair trade. The boys swapped tooth for tick and then walked in different directions.

By this time, it was quite late. Tom hurried up to the little schoolhouse and rushed in all out of breath, as if he had run the whole way. He hung his hat on a peg and threw himself into his seat with a sigh of relief. The master,[7] who had already begun the lesson, interrupted himself:

[6] tick—small insect that sucks blood from the skin of animals and people.
[7] master—teacher.

"Thomas Sawyer!"

Tom knew that when his real first name was used, it meant trouble.

"Sir!"

"Come up here. Now Thomas, why are you late again, as usual?"

Tom was about to lie as usual when he caught sight of two long pigtails of yellow hair. He instantly said: "I STOPPED TO TALK WITH HUCKLEBERRY FINN!"

> *"Now sir, go and sit with the girls! And let this be a warning to you."*

The master opened his mouth in surprise. The whole class fell silent and wondered if Tom had finally lost his mind. The master said:

"You—you did what?"

"Stopped to talk with Huckleberry Finn."

There was no mistaking the words. "Thomas Sawyer, this is the most surprising confession I have ever heard. Take off your jacket at once."

The master whacked Tom with the switch until his arm was sore. Then he said, "Now sir, go and sit with the girls! And let this be a warning to you."

Tom pretended to be upset, but this was the punishment he had been hoping for all along. He sat down upon the end of the pine bench and took a quick look at the girl with the yellow hair.

As soon as the rest of the class had stopped looking, Tom cautiously passed a peach along to the girl. She thrust it away. Tom gently put it back. She thrust it away, again, but with less anger. Tom patiently returned it to its place. Then she let it remain. Tom wrote on his slate,[8] "Please take it—I got more." The girl glanced at the words, but made no sign. Now the boy began to draw something on the slate, hiding his work with his left hand. For a time the girl refused to notice. At last, however, her curiosity got the better of her and she whispered:

"Let me see it."

Tom partly showed her a sketch of a house with a chimney. The girl gazed at it a moment and then whispered: "It's nice. Draw a man."

The artist drew a man in the front yard and she promptly whispered: "It's a beautiful man! Now draw me walking along."

Tom drew a pretty shape with a head and sticks for arms. In the hand of this figure, he placed an enormous fan. The girl said:

"It's ever so nice—I wish I could draw."

"It's easy," whispered Tom, "I'll learn you."

"Oh, will you? When?"

"At lunch time. Do you go home to eat?"

---

[8] slate—chalkboard. Each student had one to write on that was about the size of a large book.

"I'll stay, if you will."

"Good—that's a deal. What's your name?"

"Becky Thatcher. What's yours? Oh, I know. It's Thomas Sawyer."

"Well, I'm really Tom. You'll call me Tom, won't you?"

"Yes."

Then Tom began to **scrawl**[9] something on the slate, hiding the words from the girl. But she begged to see. Tom said:

"Oh, it ain't anything."

"Oh, I want to see it. Please let me."

"You'll tell."

"No I won't—deed[10] and deed and double deed I won't."

"You won't tell anybody at all?—Ever, as long as you live?"

"No I won't ever tell anybody. Now let me see."

So Tom held up his slate and let Becky read the words he had printed there: "I love you."

"O, you bad thing!" she cried, but she looked pleased just the same.

---

[9] **scrawl**—scribble.

[10] deed—slang for "indeed," meaning "for sure."

CHAPTER SIX

Heartbreak

Tom proposes to Becky, and the two become engaged. When Becky learns that Tom was engaged before, she is surprised and hurt.

At lunch time, Tom flew to Becky Thatcher and found a seat with her in the yard. Then they sat together, with a slate before them. Tom gave Becky the pencil and held her hand in his and helped her draw a house. All the while the two were talking. Tom was swimming in **bliss**.[1] He said:

"Do you love rats?"

"No! I hate them!"

"Well, I do too—live ones. But I mean dead ones, to swing around your head with a string."

---

[1] **bliss**—happiness.

"No, I don't care for rats much, anyway. What I like is chewing-gum."

"Oh, I should say so! I wish I had some now."

"Do you? I've got some. I'll let you chew it a while, but you must give it back to me."

That was fine with Tom, so they passed the piece of gum back and forth for awhile. Soon, Tom felt he had to ask:

"Say, Becky, was you ever engaged?"

"What's that?"

"Why, engaged to be married."

"No."

"Would you like to?"

"I reckon so. I don't know. What is it like?"

"Like? Why, it's wonderful. You tell a boy you won't ever have anybody but him, and then you kiss and that's all. Anybody can do it."

"Kiss? What do you kiss for?"

"Why—well, they always do that."

"Everybody?"

"Why yes, everybody that's in love with each other. Do you remember what I wrote on the slate?"

"Ye—yes."

"Well, I want to whisper it again to you."

Becky hesitated, so Tom put his arm around her waist and whispered the little sentence ever so softly, with his mouth close to her ear. And then he added:

"Now you whisper it to me—just the same."

She wouldn't do what he asked for a while, and then said: "But you mustn't ever tell anybody—will you, Tom? Now you won't, will you?"

"No, indeed I won't."

He turned his face away. She bent timidly around till her breath stirred his curls and whispered, "I—love—you!"

Then she threw her white apron over her face and ran into the classroom and hid in the corner.

Tom followed her. "Now Becky, it's all done—all but the kiss. Don't you be afraid of that—it ain't anything at all."

By and by she gave up, and Tom kissed the red lips. Then he said: "Now it's all done, Becky. And always after this, you know, you can't ever love anybody but me, and you can't ever marry anybody but me. All right?"

"All right, I'll never love anybody but you, Tom, and I'll never marry anybody but you. And you can't ever marry anybody but me, either."

"Certainly. Of course. And we can walk to school together, and choose each other at parties and everything else."

"Well, being engaged is so nice. I never heard of it before."

"Oh it's ever so **gay**![2] Why me and Amy Lawrence—"

Becky's big eyes told Tom he had just made a mistake, and he stopped, completely confused.

> *"Well, being engaged is so nice. I never heard of it before."*

"Oh, Tom! Then I ain't the first you've ever been engaged to!"

She began to cry. Tom said: "Oh don't cry, Becky, I don't care for her anymore."

"Yes you do, Tom! You know you do."

Tom tried to put his arm around Becky's neck, but she pushed him away and turned her face to the wall and went on crying. Tom tried again, but he could not comfort her. Then he became annoyed and went back outside. He stood around waiting to see if she'd come find him, but she did not. Then he began to feel badly, so he went back inside and said **hesitantly**:[3] "Becky, I—I don't care for anybody but you."

No reply—but sobs.

Tom got out his most valuable treasure, a brass knob from the top of an andiron.[4] He said: "Please, Becky, won't you take it?"

---

[2] **gay**—joyous.

[3] **hesitantly**—slowly, with pauses.

[4] andiron—one of a pair of metal supports for holding wood in a fireplace.

She struck it to the floor. Then Tom marched out of the school and far away. He would return to school no more that day.

Eventually, Becky started to worry. She called out: "Tom! Come back, Tom!"

She listened carefully, but there was no answer. So she sat down to cry again and felt angry with herself. For the rest of the afternoon, she hid her broken heart and worried about Tom.

CHAPTER SEVEN

A Pirate Bold to Be

Tom decides to go off and be a pirate. Later, Joe Harper comes upon Tom in the woods, and they play a game of Robin Hood.

Tom dodged here and there through the town until he was far away from the school. Half an hour later, he was disappearing behind the **Widow**[1] Douglas's **mansion**[2] at the top of Cardiff Hill. He entered a thick forest, picked his way to the center of it, and sat down on a mossy spot under a spreading oak. He had been here many times before.

Tom was sad to his very soul. He sat with his elbows on his knees and his chin in his hands,

---

[1] **Widow**—woman whose husband has died.

[2] **mansion**—extremely large house.

meditating.[3] It seemed to him that life was nothing but trouble. If he only had a clean Sunday-school record, he would be willing to die and be done with it all. He had been as nice as could be, and Becky had treated him like a dog. She would be sorry some day—maybe when it was too late. Ah, if he could only die **temporarily!**[4]

What if he turned his back now and disappeared mysteriously?

Tom began thinking what if he turned his back now and disappeared mysteriously? What if he went into unknown countries beyond the seas—and never came back any more! How would she feel then?

Suddenly, he had an idea. He would become a pirate! That was it! He would sail the dancing seas and people would **shudder**[5] whenever they saw him. When he was at his most famous, he would sail back to St. Petersburg and suddenly appear in the village square. When they saw him, people would whisper: "It's Tom Sawyer the Pirate!—Terror of the Seas!"

Yes, his career was decided. He would run away and become a pirate. He would set out the next morning, after he got his things together.

---

[3] **meditating**—thinking seriously and carefully.

[4] **temporarily**—for the moment; not forever.

[5] **shudder**—shiver in fear or disgust.

Just then, the blast of a toy tin trumpet came faintly down the green aisles of the forest. Tom threw off his jacket and raked away at some leaves to uncover his bow, arrow, wooden sword, and tin trumpet—all of which he kept hidden in the forest in case he needed them. He grabbed these things and bounded away. Under a great elm, he blew an answering blast and then began to tip-toe, looking carefully about. He whispered—to an imaginary group of companions:

"Hold, my merry men! Keep hid till I blow."[6]

Now appeared his best friend, Joe Harper, who was dressed and armed the same as Tom.

"Hold! Who comes here into Sherwood Forest without my permission?" Tom demanded.

"Guy of Guisborne[7] wants no man's pass. Who art thou that—that—"

"—Dares to use such language," said Tom.

"Who art thou that dares to use such language?"

"I am Robin Hood, as you shall soon know!"

They took up their wooden swords, dumped their other things onto the ground, and began **fencing**[8] in a lively way. Tom's problems were forgotten.

---

[6] "Hold, my merry men . . ."—Tom is pretending to be Robin Hood.

[7] Guy of Guisborne—one of Robin Hood's sworn enemies.

[8] **fencing**—fighting with swords.

CHAPTER EIGHT

Tragedy in the Graveyard

Huck and Tom go together to the cemetery, as promised. When they hear men coming, Tom and Huck hide behind a gravestone. From their hiding spot they see a terrible scene.

At half past nine that night, Tom and Sid were sent to bed, as usual. They said their prayers, and Sid was soon asleep.

Tom lay awake and waited impatiently for Huck's signal. Finally, he heard a faint "meow." Tom threw on his clothes, jumped out the window onto the roof, and then leapt to the ground. He meowed softly in return. Huckleberry Finn was there, just as he had promised. In his hand, he held the dead cat.

The boys moved off and disappeared into the **gloom**.[1] At the end of half an hour, they were walking through the tall grass of the graveyard. The graveyard was on a hill, about a mile and a half from the village. It was surrounded by a crazy, old, falling-down fence. Grass and weeds grew between the graves. The graves themselves were sunken into the ground. There was not a **tombstone**[2] in place. They had all fallen down over time.

A faint wind moaned through the trees, and Tom feared it might be the **spirits**[3] of the dead complaining at being disturbed. The boys didn't talk, as they were afraid of being heard by the spirits. Eventually, they found the recently dug grave they had been looking for. They hid themselves behind three great trees that grew in a bunch within a few feet of the grave.

Then they waited in silence for what seemed a long time. Finally, Tom could stand it no longer and said: "Hucky, do you believe the dead people like it for us to be here?"

---

[1] **gloom**—dark.
[2] **tombstone**—marker placed at a grave to show who is buried there.
[3] **spirits**—ghosts.

Huckleberry replied: "I wished I knowed. It's awful quiet, ain't it?"

Just then, Tom grabbed his friend's arm and said: "Shhhhh!"

"What is it, Tom?" And the two clung together with beating hearts.

"Shh! There 'tis again! Didn't you hear it?"

"Lord, Tom, they're coming! The spirits are coming! What'll we do?"

"Listen!"

The boys bent their heads together and scarcely breathed. A **muffled**[4] sound of voices floated up from the far end of the graveyard.

"Look! See there!" whispered Tom. "What is it?"

"It's a light! The spirits are giving off a light! Oh, I don't like this a bit," Huck shivered.

At last the boys could see some men approaching through the gloom, swinging an old-fashioned **lantern**[5] that was giving off a strong light. Huck took one look and whispered: "It's the devils! Three of 'em! Lordy, Tom, we're goners![6] Shh!"

"What is it, Huck?"

"They're not spirits! They're humans! One of 'em is, anyway. One of 'em has old Muff Potter's voice."

---

[4] **muffled**—softened; not clearly spoken.

[5] **lantern**—lamp.

[6] **goners**—people in danger of death.

"Are you sure?" Tom asked in surprise.

"You bet I am. And I'm sure he's too drunk to notice us. He drinks all the time, like my pap. But keep still anyway."

As the men drew closer, Tom whispered: "Huck, I know another one of them voices. It's Injun Joe."

"That's so. It *is* Injun Joe. What do you think he's doing here?"

The boys grew silent again, however, because the three men had reached Hoss Williams's grave and were standing over it.

"Here it is," said the third voice. He held the lantern up, and the boys could see the face of young Dr. Robinson.

> **"Here it is," said the third voice. He held the lantern up, and the boys could see the face of young Dr. Robinson.**

Potter and Injun Joe were carrying a wheelbarrow[7] with a rope and a couple of shovels on it. They threw down their equipment and started to dig. The doctor sat down with his back against one of the trees. He was so close that the boys could have touched him.

"Hurry, men!" he said in a low voice. "The moon might come out at any moment."

---

[7] wheelbarrow—cart with three wheels that is usually used for gardening.

They growled a response and went on digging. For some time there was no noise but the grating sound of the shovels hacking away at the dirt. Finally, a shovel struck upon the coffin with a dull wooden sound. Within another moment or two, the men had pulled the coffin up and put it on the ground.

They pried off the lid with their shovels, got out the body, and dumped it rudely on the ground. The moon drifted from behind the clouds and lit up the pale face of the corpse. Potter pushed the wheel-barrow over and the men threw the body into it. Then they covered it with a blanket and tied it into place with the rope.

"Now we've done the work, Sawbones.[8] You give us another five dollars, or we'll just leave the body here," Potter said with a growl.

"That's the idea!" said Injun Joe in agreement.

"Look here, what does this mean?" said the doctor. "You asked for your pay in advance, and I've paid you."

"Yes, and you done more than that," said Injun Joe to the doctor, who was now standing. "Five years ago, you sent me away from your father's kitchen one night, when I come to ask for something to eat. You said I warn't there for any good an'

---

[8] Sawbones—doctor. The men have dug up a body so that Dr. Robinson can experiment on it. Because there were laws against experimenting on human bodies, grave robbing was somewhat common in Twain's time.

told me to get out. And when I swore I'd get even with you if it took a hundred years, your father had me jailed for a vagrant.[9] Did you think I'd forget? Now that I've got you, you'll have to settle up."

He was threatening the doctor, with his fist in his face, by this time. The doctor struck out suddenly and threw Injun Joe on the ground. Potter dropped his knife and exclaimed: "Here, now, don't you hit my partner!"

In the next moment, he had grabbed the doctor and the two began struggling. Injun Joe sprang to his feet, his eyes flaming with anger. He snatched up Potter's knife and went creeping toward the doctor. He was looking for a chance to stab the man. All at once, the doctor flung himself free. He seized a heavy plank of wood that had been lying near the grave and cracked Potter over the head with it. At the same time, Injun Joe saw his chance and drove the knife into the doctor's chest. The doctor reeled[10] and fell upon the ground, spraying blood all over the place. Then the clouds blotted out the moon, and the two frightened boys went running off into the night.

---

[9] vagrant—tramp; unemployed, homeless person.

[10] **reeled**—turned around off balance; staggered.

When the moon came out again, Injun Joe was standing over the two forms with a strange expression on his face. The doctor murmured something, gave a long gasp, and was still. Injun Joe muttered: "That debt is paid—damn you."

Then he robbed the body. After that, he put the knife in Potter's open right hand and sat down on the ground to wait.

Three—four—five minutes passed, and then Potter began to stir and moan. His hand closed upon the knife. He raised it, glanced at it, and then let it fall with a shudder. Next he sat up, pushing the body from him, and gazed at it with confusion. His eyes met Joe's.

"Lord, what happened here, Joe?" he said.

"It's a dirty business," said Joe, without moving. "What did you do it for?"

"I! I done nothing!"

"Look here! That kind of talk won't work."

Potter trembled and grew white. "I'm all in a **muddle**,[11] Joe. I can't remember anything hardly. Tell me, Joe—honest, now, old feller—did I do it? Joe, I never meant to—upon my soul and honor, I never meant to. Tell me what happened, Joe. Oh, it's awful—and him so young and **promising**."[12]

---

[11] **muddle**—confused state.

[12] **promising**—seeming to have a successful future.

"Why, you two was fighting. He hit you over the head with a board, and you fell flat. Then you come up with a knife in your hand and jammed it into him, just as he hit you over the head again. You fell to the ground with him on top of you and here you've laid, dead as a door, till now," Joe made this explanation to Muff, who sat with a horrified look on his face.

"I never used a weapon in my life before, Joe. I've fought, but never with weapons."

"Oh, I didn't know what I was a-doing!" he exclaimed. It was all because of the whisky and the excitement, I reckon. I never used a weapon in my life before, Joe. I've fought, but never with weapons. Say you won't tell, Joe—that's a good feller. I always liked you Joe, and stood up for you, too. Don't you remember? You won't tell, will you Joe?"

"You've always been fair and square with me, Muff Potter, and I won't tell on you."

"Oh, Joe, you're an angel. I'll bless you for this every day I live." And Potter began to cry.

"Come, now, that's enough of that. This ain't any time for blubbering. You go now and I'll fix this mess. Move, now, and don't leave any tracks behind you."

Potter started out on a trot that quickly increased to a run. Injun Joe stood looking after him. He muttered: "He's forgotten about the knife. He won't dare come back for it if he does remember, the chicken-heart!"

Two or three minutes later, Injun Joe himself left. The murdered man, the blanketed corpse, the coffin, and the open grave lay there for all to see.

CHAPTER NINE

An Oath and More Heartbreak

Tom and Huck run away from the graveyard. They discuss what they saw and decide that Injun Joe will come after them if they tell.

The two boys ran on and on toward the village. Speechless with horror, they glanced backward over their shoulders from time to time to see if they were being followed.

"If we can only get to the old tannery[1] before we break down!" whispered Tom, in short catches between breaths. "I can't run much farther."

Huckleberry's hard pantings were his only reply, and the boys kept running toward the tannery.

---

[1] tannery—factory where animal hides are made into leather.

Steadily they gained on it until at last they burst through the open door and fell gratefully to the floor. When their hearts stopped racing, Tom whispered: "Huckleberry, what do you reckon will come of this?"

"If Dr. Robinson dies, I reckon someone'll be hanged for the crime."

Tom thought a while. Then he said: "Who'll tell? Will we?"

"Are you crazy? Injun Joe'd kill us in an instant."

"That's just what I was thinking to myself, Huck."

"If anybody tells, let Muff Potter do it," Huck suggested.

Tom said nothing, but he went on thinking. Presently he whispered: "Huck, Muff Potter don't know what happened. He was lying there when Injun Joe stabbed the doctor. How could he know anything?"

"By hokey, that's so, Tom!"

After another deep silence, Tom said: "Hucky, you sure you can keep mum?"[2]

"Tom, we got to keep mum. You know that. So look-a-here. Let's swear to one another. We'll swear to keep quiet."

---

[2] keep mum—stay quiet, not talk about it.

"I'm agreed, Huck. It's the best thing. I swear that we—"

"O, no, that swear won't work for something like this. It's too weak. We got to swear with blood."

Tom loved this idea. It was deep, and dark, and awful. He picked up a clean pine shingle that lay in the moonlight, took a little fragment of coal from his pocket, and wrote:

Huck Finn and Tom Sawyer Swears They Will Keep Mum about This and They Wish They may Drop down dead in Their Tracks if They ever Tell and Rot.

> **Then Tom pulled a needle from his sleeve, and each boy pricked the ball of his thumb and squeezed out a drop of blood.**

Huckleberry was filled with admiration when he saw Tom's skill as a writer.

Then Tom pulled a needle from his sleeve, and each boy pricked the ball of his thumb and squeezed out a drop of blood. In time, after many squeezes, Tom managed to sign his initials, using the ball of his little finger for a pen. Then he showed Huckleberry how to make an *H* and an *F,* and the oath[3] was complete.

The boys separated after further promises to keep quiet. When Tom crept back in his bedroom

---

[3] **oath**—promise.

window, it was almost morning. He undressed carefully, relieved that no one had noticed he was gone. He was not aware that the gently snoring Sid was awake, and had been so for an hour.

When Tom awoke, Sid was dressed and gone. The sun was high, and he was startled. Why hadn't Aunt Polly called him? The thought filled him with worry. He dressed quickly and rushed down to breakfast. The family was still at the table, but no one would look at him. He sat down and tried to act cheerful, but he couldn't get a smile or a response.

After breakfast, his aunt took him aside. She cried over him and asked him how he could break her old heart so. She finally told him to go on to school, and he felt terrible about all the trouble he had caused her. He'd rather that she had gone and whipped him. The tears were too much for him to bear.

At school, the schoolmaster whipped him and Joe Harper for playing hooky the day before. When he got to his desk, he saw an object all wrapped up in paper. With a sad heart, he unwrapped the thing. It was his brass andiron knob! Becky had returned it to him.

This final straw broke the camel's back. Tom sunk his head to his desk and wanted to cry.

CHAPTER TEN

Tom Feels Guilty

*The entire village is talking about the murder of
Dr. Robinson. Muff Potter is quickly arrested for the
crime. Tom feels terrible that Muff is in jail for a
crime he did not commit.*

At noon the next day, the whole village was suddenly **electrified**[1] with the terrible news. The story flew from man to man, from group to group, and from house to house. The school closed for the afternoon because an important man of the village had been murdered.

A bloody knife had been found close to the murdered man, and it had been recognized by somebody as belonging to Muff Potter.

---
[1] **electrified**—very excited.

It was also said that the town had been searched for this "murderer," but that he could not be found.

Men checked all roads in every direction, and the Sheriff "was sure" that the man would be arrested before night.

He turned, and his eyes met Huckleberry's.

All the people in the town were making their way toward the grave-yard. Tom's worries disappeared and he joined the group, even though the graveyard was the last place on earth he wanted to be. Still, he was curious. As soon as he arrived at the graveyard, he wormed[2] his way through the crowd and saw the horrible sight. As he was looking, somebody pinched his arm. He turned, and his eyes met Huckleberry's. Then they both looked away and wondered if anyone had noticed.

"Poor fellow!" "Poor young fellow!" "This ought to be a lesson to grave-robbers!" "Muff Potter'll hang for this if they catch him!" This was what people were saying.

Suddenly Tom shivered from head to toe, for his eye fell upon the dark face of Injun Joe. At this moment the crowd began to sway and move. Voices shouted, "It's him! It's him! He's coming himself! Muff Potter is coming!"

---

[2] wormed—squeezed.

The crowd fell apart, now, and the Sheriff came through, leading Potter by the arm. The poor fellow's face was **haggard**,[3] and his eyes showed his fear. When he stood before the murdered man, his whole body shook. He put his face in his hands and burst into tears.

"I didn't do it, friends," he sobbed. "Upon my word and honor, I never done it."

"Is this your knife?" the Sheriff asked in an angry voice.

Potter would have fallen if they had not caught him and laid him on the ground. Then he said: "Something told me that I should come back and get that knife! But I couldn't! I was too scared! Tell 'em, Joe. Tell 'em—it ain't any use any more."

Then Huckleberry and Tom stood silent and staring and heard Injun Joe, the liar, tell his false story. And when he had finished, Tom and Huck looked at the ground. Clearly this man—this Injun Joe—had sold himself to Satan.[4] It would be fatal to mess with him.

---

[3] **haggard**—worn and tired.
[4] Satan—the devil.

Tom's **conscience**[5] disturbed his sleep for as much as a week after this. At breakfast one morning, Sid said: "Tom, you roll around and talk in your sleep so much that you keep me awake."

Tom turned white as a ghost and dropped his eyes.

"It's a bad sign," said Aunt Polly, seriously. "What you got on your mind, Tom?"

"Nothing. Nothing that I know of." But the boy's hand shook so that he spilled his coffee.

"And you do say such strange things," Sid said. "Last night you said 'It's blood, it's blood, that's what it is!'"

"And you do say such strange things," Sid said. "Last night you said 'It's blood, it's blood, that's what it is!' You said that over and over. And you said, 'Don't torment me so—I'll tell!' Tell what? What is it you'll tell?"

Everything was swimming before Tom. There is no saying what might have happened, but luckily the worry passed out of Aunt Polly's face and she came to Tom's rescue without knowing it. She said: "Oh! It's that awful murder. I dream about it most every night myself. Sometimes I dream it's me that done it."

---

[5] **conscience**—inner feelings and ideas that tell a person what is right and wrong.

Mary said she had been affected much the same way. Sid seemed satisfied. That same night, Tom began complaining of a toothache and tied up his jaws before he went to sleep. He did this for a week. He never knew that Sid lay watching him every night. Many times, Sid slipped the bandage free and then listened to what a dreaming Tom had to say.

Every day or two during this time of sadness, Tom waited for his chance and then went to the little jail-window and sneaked in bits of food and other necessities to the "murderer." These errands greatly helped to ease Tom's conscience, which bothered him constantly.

The villagers had a strong desire to tar-and-feather[6] Injun Joe and run him out of town because of his role in the grave-robbing, but most people were sort of afraid of him. No one was willing to take the lead in the matter, so at last it was dropped, and people decided to leave Injun Joe alone.

---

[6] tar-and-feather—punish by pouring hot tar on a person and then rolling the person in feathers.

CHAPTER ELEVEN

The Cat and the Pain-Killer

Tom mopes because he's upset about Becky. Aunt Polly decides to try some medicine on him to see if it will help.

For awhile, at least, Tom was able to almost forget about the murder. He had other things to think about—Becky Thatcher, for example. Much to Tom's disappointment, Becky had stopped coming to school.

Tom started hanging around outside her father's house, hoping he would see the girl. He learned that she was sick. What if she should die! He was terrified at the thought. He no longer was interested in being a pirate. Life had gone sour. There was no more fun for Tom.

He put his toys away, and his bat, since there was no joy in them any more. His aunt was worried. She began to try all kinds of remedies[1] on him. She was one of those people who loved patent medicines[2] and was always first in line to buy a new one.

Early each morning, she stood him up in the woodshed and drowned him with a bucketful of cold water.

One of her "Health" journals had lately discussed the wonders of the "water treatment." Aunt Polly decided this was just the thing to help Tom. Early each morning, she stood him up in the woodshed and drowned him with a bucketful of cold water. Then she scrubbed him down with a damp towel, rolled him up in a wet sheet, and put him away under blankets until she had "sweated his soul clean."

In spite of the water treatments, however, the boy grew sadder and more sick-looking. Aunt Polly added hot baths, shower baths, and hose baths. The boy remained as grim as a hearse.[3] She put him on an oatmeal diet and wrapped him up in bandages

---

[1] remedies—cures.
[2] patent medicines—nonprescription drugs.
[3] hearse—car used to carry dead bodies to the grave.

each night. Every day she went to work on him with a new quack[4] cure.

Tom hardly said a word about these treatments. That's how sad he was. His **indifference**[5] filled the old lady's heart with worry. She ordered a case of a new medicine called Pain-Killer. When it arrived, she tasted a drop. It tasted worse than anything she had ever had. This would wake the boy up! She gave him a teaspoonful and was satisfied when the boy screamed as if she had built a fire under him.

By and by, Tom felt that it was time to pull himself together. This sort of life was becoming a little dull. He didn't know what to do about the Pain-Killer, though. He knew Aunt Polly would make him keep taking it, no matter what. So he came up with a plan. He would pretend to *like* the taste of Pain-Killer!

Tom started asking for the awful stuff so often that he became a pest, and his aunt ended up telling him to help himself and quit bothering her. So every once in a while he poured a bit from the bottle into a crack in the sitting room floor. Aunt Polly, who carefully watched the level of medicine

---

[4] quack—fake medical.
[5] **indifference**—lack of concern.

in the bottle, was happy to see that it was disappearing just as it should.

One day Tom was in the act of pouring the medicine down the crack when his aunt's yellow cat came along. The cat eyed the teaspoon and begged for a taste. Tom said: "Don't ask for it unless you want it, Peter."

But Peter showed that he *did* want it.

"You better make sure."

Peter was sure.

"Now you've asked for it, and I'll give it to you, Peter, because there ain't nothing mean about me. But if you find you don't like it, don't blame anybody but your own self."

Peter thought this was fine. So Tom pried the cat's mouth open and poured down the Pain-Killer. Peter jumped a couple of feet into the air and then delivered a war-whoop and set off round and round the room. He banged against furniture, turned over flower pots, and made a terrible mess. Next he rose on his **hind**[6] feet and danced around, meowing like crazy. Aunt Polly came in the room just in time to see Peter spin around in the air, give

---

[6] **hind**—back.

out a final screech, and then jump through the open window. The old lady was shocked. Tom lay on the floor howling with laughter.

"Tom, what on earth is wrong with that cat?"

"I don't know, Aunt," gasped the boy.

"Why, I've never see anything like it. What made him act that way?"

"Indeed I don't know, Aunt Polly. Cats always act that way when they're having a good time."

"They do, do they?" There was something in her tone of voice that made Tom feel worried.

"Yes'm. That is, I believe they do."

"You do?"

"Yes'm."

The old lady was bending down to pull the teaspoon out from under the bed. Polly held it up, stared at Tom, and then gave him a good, hard crack on the head with her **thimble**.[7]

"Now, sir, why did you give that medicine to that poor dumb animal?"

"I done it out of pity for him because he doesn't have an aunt."

"Doesn't have an aunt! You fool! What has that got to do with it?"

---

[7] **thimble**—small metal cap worn on a finger to protect it from the needle when sewing.

"Loads. Because if he'd a had one, she would have cured him with the water treatment, towels, sheets, blankets, and Pain-Killer. I did it because he had no one else to help him along."

Aunt Polly felt a sudden pang of **remorse**.[8] This was putting the thing in a new light. After all, what was awful for a cat might be awful for a boy, too. She began to feel sorry.

He hung around at the gate just as he did each day, hoping to see Becky Thatcher walking down the street toward school.

Her eyes watered a little, and she put her hand on Tom's head. She said gently: "I was meaning for the best, Tom. And Tom, it did do you good."

Tom looked up in her face with just a little twinkle in his eye. He replied: "I know you was meaning for the best, Auntie, and so was I with Peter. It done him good, too. I never see him move so quickly since—"

"O, go 'long with you, Tom, before you **aggravate**[9] me again. And you try and see if you can be a good boy, for once, so you don't need to take any more medicine."

---

[8] **remorse**—regret.
[9] **aggravate**—annoy.

Tom reached school ahead of time. He hung around at the gate just as he did each day, hoping to see Becky Thatcher walking down the street toward school. Today he saw her for the first time in weeks, and his heart jumped in his chest. The next instant he was running about, yelling, laughing, chasing boys, throwing handsprings, and all kinds of other brave things all in the hopes that Becky would notice him. But she seemed to be ignoring him. She never even looked. Could it be that she had not seen him? He moved closer to her and began fooling around just a few feet away from where she was standing. Without even looking at him, she walked away with her nose in the air. He heard her say: "Mf! Some people think they're mighty smart—always showing off!"

Tom's cheeks burned. He gathered himself up and sneaked off, completely crushed.

CHAPTER TWELVE

The Pirate Crew Sets Sail

Tom feels so unloved that he decides to run away and be a pirate. Joe Harper and Huck join him on the adventure. They make a camp on Jackson's Island.

Tom's mind was made up now. He felt desperate. He was a **forsaken**,[1] friendless boy. He had been turned away by Aunt Polly and Becky both. Nobody loved him or cared about him. The only thing they wanted was to be rid of him, so he would do as they wished. They had forced him to it at last. He would lead a life of crime. There was no other choice.

---

[1] **forsaken**—abandoned.

Slowly he walked away from school. In the distance, he heard the school bell ring, and he sobbed to think he would never hear that old familiar sound again. It was very hard, what he was about to do, but it had been forced upon him.

Wiping his eyes with his sleeve, Tom began to tell Joe about his troubles.

At that moment, he met his friend Joe Harper walking along. Joe looked as unhappy as Tom felt. Wiping his eyes with his sleeve, Tom began to tell Joe about his troubles. He explained that he was going to travel around the world and never return home. He hoped that Joe would not forget him.

But it turned out that this was exactly what Joe himself was planning to do, and had come looking for Tom in order to say good-bye. His mother had whipped him for drinking some cream that he had never touched. It was plain to Joe that his mother was tired of him and wished him to go away. Joe decided that he had no other choice but to leave at once.

As the two boys walked along, they made a new **pact**[2] to stand by each other and never separate till death ended all their troubles. Then they began to make their plans.

---

[2] **pact**—agreement.

Three miles below St. Petersburg, at a point where the Mississippi River was just over a mile wide, there was a long, narrow, island that was almost all woods. The island, on which nobody lived, was called Jackson's Island. Tom and Joe decided they would make this their new home.

Then they hunted up Huckleberry Finn, and he joined them promptly, for any career was fine with him. The boys separated and agreed to meet on the river bank that night at midnight. There was a small log raft there that they could use as their boat. They would bring fishing gear and as many supplies as they could pull together.

Around midnight, Tom arrived at the meeting place with a boiled ham and some cornmeal. The night was starry and very still. The mighty river lay like an ocean at rest. Tom listened a moment, but he heard no sound. Then he gave a low, clear whistle. It was answered from a little way over. Tom whistled twice more. These signals were answered in the same way. Then a **guarded**[3] voice asked:

"Who goes there?"

"Tom Sawyer, the Black Avenger[4] of the Spanish Main.[5] Name your names."

---

[3] **guarded**—cautious.

[4] Avenger—person who seeks revenge.

[5] Spanish Main—section of the Caribbean Sea crossed by Spanish ships in colonial times.

"Huck Finn the Red-Handed, and Joe Harper the Terror of the Seas."[6]

"Good. Give the signal."

Two hoarse whispers delivered the same awful word at the same time to the quiet night:

"BLOOD!"

Two hoarse whispers delivered the same awful word at the same time to the quiet night:

"BLOOD!"

Then Tom threw his ham over the river bank and let himself down after it, tearing both skin and clothes a bit along the way. There was an easy, comfortable path to the bank that he might have used, but no good pirate would have thought of using it.

The Terror of the Seas had brought along a huge chunk of bacon. Finn the Red-Handed had stolen a frying pan and some leaf tobacco. He had also brought a few corn-cobs to make pipes with, although none of the pirates smoked but himself.

As soon as they had their raft ready, the boys shoved off with Tom in command, Huck at the oar, and Joe at the rear. Tom stood with arms folded and gave orders in a low, important-sounding whisper:

"Bring her to the wind!"

---

[6] "Huck Finn . . . Seas"—The boys have chosen names from two books about pirates that were popular in the mid- to late-1800s.

"Aye-aye, sir!"

"Steady, stead-y-y-y!"

"Steady it is, sir!"

"Shake out the sails, my hearties!" (There were no sails, of course, except an old torn one that lay in the bottom of the raft.)

"Aye-aye, sir!"

The raft moved slowly past St. Petersburg. Two or three glimmering lights showed where the village lay, peacefully sleeping, beyond the huge sweep of star-gemmed water. The Black Avenger stood, his arms still folded, and "looked his last" upon the scene of all his joys and sufferings. Although Jackson's Island was actually within view of the town, Tom chose to ignore this fact and felt certain that he'd never see the village again.

The other pirates took a last look also. In fact, they all looked so long that they nearly allowed the current to take them out of range of Jackson's Island. But they figured out what was happening just in time, and were able to turn the raft around.

At about two o'clock in the morning, the raft landed on a little sand-bar[7] at the edge of the island.

---

[7] sand-bar—ridge of sand in shallow water.

The boys waded back and forth until they had unloaded all their supplies. Then they took the torn sail from the bottom of the raft and hung it over a bush. This would be a tent to protect their food. The pirates, of course, would sleep in the open air.

The pirates, of course, would sleep in the open air.

They built a fire and cooked some bacon in the frying-pan for supper and used up half of the cornmeal they had brought. It was a wonderful meal and the boys enjoyed every moment of it. When the last crisp slice of bacon was gone, the boys stretched themselves out on the grass. All three were filled with happiness.

"Ain't this gay?" said Joe.

"You bet!" said Tom. "What would our friends say if they could see us?"

"Say? Well they'd just about die to be here, right Hucky?"

"I reckon so," said Huckleberry. "This suits me fine. I got plenty to eat and no one to bother me."

"Right," said Tom. "We don't have to get up early in the morning, wash our faces, and go to school. This is much better than being a **hermit**,[8] Joe."

"O yes, that's so," said Joe.

---

[8] hermit—person who lives alone and far from society.

Gradually their talk died out and they began to feel sleepy. The Red-Handed fell asleep right away because he had no cares or worries to keep him awake. But the Terror of the Seas and the Black Avenger of the Spanish Main had more trouble getting to sleep. Their consciences were keeping them awake. They began to worry that they had done wrong to steal the meat and run away. They worried about this problem for a while. Then each boy's conscience gave up for the night, and the pirates were able to fall into a contented sleep.

CHAPTER THIRTEEN

Happy Camp of the Pirates

The boys spend a joyful day on the island. They watch as the town of St. Petersburg searches high and low for them. Tom, Joe, and Huck feel a little homesick, but not one of them will admit it.

When Tom awoke in the morning, he wondered where he was. He sat up and rubbed his eyes and looked around. Then he remembered. It was a cool gray dawn, and the woods were deliciously silent. Beaded dew-drops stood upon the leaves and grasses. A white layer of ashes covered the fire, and a thin blue breath of smoke rose straight into the air.

Tom woke up the other pirates, and in a minute or two they had pulled their clothes off and were heading for the river. They no longer felt any longing for the little village sleeping in the distance. A small current had carried away their raft, but this only made them feel happier, since it meant that the last bridge between them and civilization was now gone.

They no longer felt any longing for the little village sleeping in the distance.

After their swim, they came back to camp feeling glad-hearted and starving. Soon they had the camp-fire blazing again. Huck found a spring of clear, cold water close by, and the boys made cups out of big oak leaves. While Joe was slicing bacon for breakfast, Tom and Huck threw their fishing lines into the river and caught a couple of handsome catfish.

They fried the fish with the bacon and decided that no fish had ever tasted so good before. After breakfast, they lay around in the shade for a bit and then went off exploring in the woods.

They discovered that the island was about three miles long and a quarter of a mile wide, and that the shore it lay closest to [the Illinois shore] was only separated from it by a narrow **channel**[1] that was two hundred yards wide.

---

[1] **channel**—part of a river deep enough for ships to pass through.

They took a swim about every hour, so it was close upon the middle of the afternoon when they got back to camp. They were too hungry to stop to fish, so they ate the cold ham and then lay in the shade to talk.

Soon, however, the talk began to drag and then die out all together. The stillness of the woods began to affect the spirits of the boys. A kind of longing came over all three of them. Soon they realized it for what it was: homesickness. No one said a word, however, because no one wanted to be called weak by the others.

Around this time, the boys heard a strange sound in the distance. The boys started, glanced at each other, and then each listened carefully. There was a long silence, heavy and unbroken. Then there was a deep BOOM that came floating down out of the distance.

"What is it?" exclaimed Joe, under his breath.

"I wonder," said Tom in a whisper.

"It ain't thunder," said Huckleberry, in a quiet tone.

They waited a bit and then they heard the same muffled boom.

"Let's go and see."

They jumped to their feet and hurried to the shore that faced St. Petersburg. They parted the

bushes on the bank and peered out over the water.
The little steam **ferryboat**[2] was about a mile below
the village, drifting with the
current. Her broad deck was
crowded with people. There
were a great many **skiffs**[3] rowing about or floating nearby,
but the boys couldn't figure
out what they were doing.
Every once in awhile, a great
jet of white smoke burst from
the ferryboat's side. As the smoke spread and rose
in a lazy cloud, the boys heard that same dull throb
of sound.

Every once in awhile, a great jet of white smoke burst from the ferryboat's side.

"I know now!" exclaimed Tom. "Somebody's
drownded!"

"That's it!" said Huck. "They done that last
summer, when Bill Turner got drownded. They
shoot a cannon over the water, and that makes the
body come up to the top."[4]

"Yes, I've heard about that," said Joe. "By jings!
I wish I was over there now," said Joe.

---

[2] **ferryboat**—boat that carries people a short distance for a small price.

[3] **skiffs**—small sailing boats.

[4] When Twain was a boy, people believed that the boom from a cannon was
capable of bursting a sunken corpse's gall bladder, which would cause it to
float to the surface.

"I do too," said Huck. "I'd give heaps to know who it is."

The boys listened and watched. Presently a thought flashed through Tom's mind, and he exclaimed: "Boys, I know who's drownded—it's us!"

They felt like heroes in an instant. Here was their triumph! They were missed, and people were sad about it. Hearts were breaking on their account. Tears were being shed, and they were the talk of the whole town. This was fine indeed!

As **twilight**[5] drew on, the ferryboat went back to her usual business, and the skiffs disappeared. The pirates returned to camp. They were excited about all the trouble they were causing. They caught fish, cooked supper, and ate it. Then they started guessing what people were saying about them.

But when the shadows of night closed in on them, they stopped talking and sat thinking. The excitement was gone, now, and Tom and Joe could not help wondering about certain people at home who were not enjoying this day as much as they were. By and by, Joe timidly said that he might like to go home sometime soon, and how did the others feel—

---

[5] **twilight**—dusk; the half light of late afternoon/early evening.

Tom put a stop to that talk right away. Huck, who didn't care where he went, helped convince Joe that he had to stay. Joe agreed and felt bad to have shown his homesickness.

As the night deepened, Huck fell asleep. Joe followed next. Tom lay upon his elbow, watching the two intently. At last he got up quietly, on his knees, and went searching among the grass. He picked up and inspected large pieces of white bark and finally chose two that seemed right. Then he knelt by the fire and painfully wrote something upon each of these with a little stub of pencil. One he rolled up and put in his jacket pocket, and the other he put in Joe's hat and placed it a little distance from the owner. When he was finished, he tip-toed his way cautiously among the trees till he was sure that he was out of hearing, and then he broke into a fast run in the direction of the sand-bar.

CHAPTER FOURTEEN

Tom's Sneaky Visit Home

Tom worries that Aunt Polly is brokenhearted. He sneaks back home to give her a note that says he is safe.

A few minutes later, Tom was in the little channel, wading his way toward the Illinois shore. When it got too deep to wade, he began swimming. The current carried him downstream a bit, but in time he reached the riverbank. He drew himself out of the water and then began walking back up the shore.

Everything was quiet under the blinking stars. He crept along until he came to the ferryboat. Moving quietly, he climbed into the boat and lay down in the back.

Presently the captain of the boat gave the order to "cast off." A minute or two later, the voyage across the river had begun. At the end of a long twelve or fifteen minutes, the boat stopped, and Tom slipped overboard and swam ashore. He pulled himself out of the river again and found himself near the edge of St. Petersburg.

There sat Aunt Polly, Sid, Mary, and Joe Harper's mother, grouped together and talking.

He ran along back streets and shortly found himself at his aunt's back fence. He climbed over the fence and peeped in the sitting-room window. There sat Aunt Polly, Sid, Mary, and Joe Harper's mother, grouped together and talking. The had their backs to the window and the door. Tom lifted the latch and opened the door very quietly. Then he tiptoed in behind them. He hid himself under Aunt Polly's bed and listened to what they were saying.

"But he warn't bad," said Aunt Polly. "He was just **mischievous**.[1] He never meant any harm, and he was the best-hearted boy that ever was"—and she began to cry.

"It was just so with my Joe," said Mrs. Harper. "He was always up to every kind of mischief, but

---

[1] **mischievous**—in trouble in a harmless way.

he was just as unselfish and kind as he could be. And dear me, to think that I went and whipped him for taking that cream, never once remembering that I had throwed it out myself because it was sour! And now I'll never see that poor, poor, boy again!" And Mrs. Harper sobbed as if her heart would break.

"I hope Tom's better off where he is," said Sid, "but if he'd been better in some ways—"

"Sid!" Aunt Polly exclaimed. "I won't hear a word against my Tom! God'll take care of him, don't you worry about that! Oh, Mrs. Harper, I don't know how to give him up, I don't know how to give him up! He was such a comfort to me, although he **tormented**[2] my old heart out of me."

"Oh, it's so hard!" Mrs. Harper replied. "Only last Saturday my Joe set off a fire-cracker right under my nose, and I knocked him to the ground. Oh, I feel terrible about it."

"Yes, yes, yes, I know just how you feel, Mrs. Harper. Yesterday afternoon, my Tom filled the cat full of Pain-Killer. And God forgive me, I cracked his head with my thimble, poor boy, poor dead boy." Then the lady broke down entirely.

Tom could hear Mary crying too. He began to have a better opinion of himself than ever before.

---

[2] **tormented**—overly annoyed.

He was so touched by his aunt's grief that he wanted to jump out from under the bed and give her a hug, but he stopped himself and lay still.

He went on listening, and soon understood that people thought the boys had drowned while they were swimming. In the beginning, there was hope that the boys might show up alive one town over. When they didn't, the whole village began to fear the worst. This was Wednesday night. If the boys weren't found, there would be a funeral on Sunday morning.

Mrs. Harper sobbed goodnight to the group and turned to go. Polly sent Sid and Mary to bed and then knelt down to say a prayer for Tom. She spoke in such a sad and trembling voice that Tom himself was crying before she was done.

Tom waited until he was sure she was asleep, and then crawled out from under the bed. He stood by her side then and watched her sleep. His heart was full of pity for her. He took out his white bark roll and placed it by the candle. But something occurred[3] to him and he paused, deep in thought.

Suddenly, his face lit up with a happy solution to the whole problem. He put the bark quickly back

---

[3] **occurred**—came as an idea.

in his pocket. He bent over, kissed Aunt Polly's faded lips, and sneaked back out of the house.

Tom made his way back to the ferry landing and saw that no one was there. He quickly untied a little skiff, slipped into it, and was soon rowing quietly back to Jackson's Island.

CHAPTER FIFTEEN

Storm in the Night

Back at the camp, Tom keeps his idea a secret. The boys play for awhile and then Joe announces that he's going home. Huck wants to go, too. To stop them, Tom tells about his plan.

Later that day, the three boys went out to hunt for turtle eggs on the sand-bar. They had a fried-egg feast that night and another on Friday morning.

After breakfast, they went whooping and running out on the bar and chased each other round and round. Every now and then they stopped to splash in the water.

When they were tired, they would run out and lay on the dry, hot sand. They played circus for a long while and then marbles for even longer. Later, the boys were tired and ready to rest. They slowly wandered apart, and all three began gazing longingly across the wide river to where the village lay **drowsing**[1] in the sun.

He needed something to get his mind off home.

Tom found himself writing "BECKY" in the sand with his big toe. He scratched it out and was angry with himself for his weakness. But he wrote it again, nevertheless. It seemed he couldn't help himself. So he went off to find the other boys. He needed something to get his mind off home.

But Joe's spirits had gotten much worse. He was so homesick that he could hardly stand it. The tears lay very near the surface. Huck was sad, too. Tom was also sad, but he tried hard not to show it. He had a secret he was not ready to tell yet, but if things continued this way, he'd have to share it. He said, with a great show of cheerfulness:

"I bet there've been pirates on this island before, boys. Let's look for some buried treasure."

But Joe and Huck had no energy for it. Tom tried one or two other ideas, but nothing worked. Finally Joe said: "Oh, boys, let's give it up. I want to go home. It's so lonesome here."

---

[1] **drowsing**—sleeping lightly.

"Oh, shucks!" Tom cried. "You're a baby! You want to see your mother, I reckon."

"Yes, I do want to see my mother—and you would too, if you had one." And then Joe sniffled a little.

"Well, we'll let the cry-baby go home to his mother, won't we, Huck? You like it here, don't you Huck? We'll stay, won't we?"

Huck said "Y-e-s," but he didn't sound sure of it.

"I'll never speak to you again as long as I live, Tom" said Joe, rising. Then he moved away from the two and began getting dressed.

"Who cares!" said Tom. "Nobody wants you to. Go 'long home and get laughed at."

But Tom was worried, nevertheless, and was alarmed to see Joe go on dressing as if no one had spoken. And then Huck said: "I want to go, too, Tom. It's getting so lonesome here. Let's us go too, Tom."

"I won't! You can all go, if you want to. I'm going to stay."

"Tom, I better go," Huck replied.

"Well go 'long—who's stopping you?"

Huck started sadly away, and Tom stood looking after him. He wanted to go too, but he knew he couldn't. He kept hoping that the boys would stop, but they waded on. It suddenly dawned on Tom that it was becoming very lonely and quiet on the island. He ran after his friends, yelling:

"Wait! Wait! I want to tell you something!"

"Wait! Wait! I want to tell you something!"

Huck and Joe stopped and turned around. When Tom got to where they were, he began unfolding his secret, and they listened until at last they saw the "point" he was driving at. When they finally understood, they set up a war-whoop of applause and said it was a "splendid idea!" They said that if he had told them at first, they wouldn't have started away.

The lads came gaily back to camp and went at their games again with all kinds of enthusiasm, chattering all the time about Tom's wonderful plan. After an egg and fish dinner, Tom said he wanted to learn to smoke. Joe said he would like to try, too. So Huck made pipes and filled them. Then the boys began puffing away. The smoke had a terrible taste to it, and they choked a little.

The boys smoked and talked about how their friends would envy them for being so bold. But presently the talk began to slow down a little. The silences widened, and Tom and Joe started looking very pale and miserable. Joe finally dropped his pipe down, and Tom did the same. Joe said feebly: "I've lost my knife. I reckon I better go and find it."

Tom said, with a tiny voice: "I'll help you. You go over that way and I'll hunt around by the water."

An hour later, Huck went to find his friends. They were wide apart in the woods, both very pale, and both fast asleep. But something told him that the two had been very sick right before they had fallen asleep.

CHAPTER SIXTEEN

Pirates at Their Own Funeral

Tom, Joe, and Huck watch their own funeral.

Meanwhile, in St. Petersburg, there was no cheerfulness to be found. The Harpers and Aunt Polly's family were dressed all in black that Saturday and had spent much of the day crying.

When the Sunday-school hour was finished the next morning, the bell began to **toll**,[1] instead of ringing in the usual way. It was a very still Sunday, and the bell seemed as **somber**[2] as the rest of the world. The villagers began to gather, stopping for a

---

[1] **toll**—ring slowly.
[2] **somber**—gloomy.

moment in the church doorway to whisper about the sad event.

No one could remember when the little church had been so full before. Finally, Aunt Polly entered, followed by Sid and Mary. The Harper family, all wearing black, came along behind them. Then there was another silence, broken only by the sound of muffled sobs. Then the minister spread his hands and prayed. A sad hymn was sung, and the service began.

No one could remember when the little church had been so full before.

Around this time, there was a rustle in the back, which nobody noticed. Several minutes later, the church door creaked open. The minister raised his red eyes and stood **transfixed**![3]

First one and then another pair of eyes followed the minister's. Then, almost with one movement, everyone in the church rose and stared while the three dead boys came marching up the aisle. Tom was in the lead, Joe came next, and Huck, in his torn rags, snuck along behind them. They had been hiding in the back, listening to their own funeral!

---

[3] **transfixed**—frozen.

Aunt Polly, Mary, and the Harpers threw themselves upon their **restored**[4] ones, covered them with kisses, and poured out their thanks.

Then the minister shouted at the top of his voice: "Praise God from whom all blessings flow! SING, my friends! And put your hearts into it!"

And they did. The villagers sang so loudly that their voices shook the roof. Tom Sawyer the Pirate looked at the jealous children around him and confessed in his heart that this was the proudest moment of his life.

---

[4] **restored**—returned.

CHAPTER SEVENTEEN

Tom Reveals His Dream Secret

Tom explains the boys' adventure on Jackson's Island and tells Aunt Polly that he dreamt of her while he was away. Because he's now "famous," Tom decides to play hard-to-get with Becky. She comes up with her own plan to get him back.

That had been Tom's great secret—the plan to return home with his brother pirates in order to watch their own funerals. They had paddled over to the Missouri shore on a log on Saturday evening and landed five or six miles below the village. They had slept in the woods at the edge of the town until nearly daylight. Then they made their way to the church and had hidden there until the funeral began.

At breakfast Monday morning, Aunt Polly and Mary were very loving to Tom and did whatever they could for him. There was an unusual amount of talk. In the course of it, Aunt Polly said: "Well, it was a fine joke, Tom, to keep everybody suffering almost a week while you boys had a good time, but it is a pity you could be so hard-hearted as to let me grieve so. If you could come over on a log to go to your funeral, you could have come over and given me a hint that you warn't dead."

> **"You could have come over and given me a hint that you warn't dead."**

"Well, I don't know. It would have spoiled everything," Tom replied.

"Tom, I wish you had loved me enough to think of it," said Aunt Polly in a tone that made the boy uncomfortable.

"Now Auntie, you know I care for you," said Tom.

"Well, you don't act like it."

"I wish now I'd thought about doing what you said," said Tom, with a sorry tone. "But I dreamed about you anyway. That's something, ain't it?"

"Well, it ain't much, but it's better than nothing. What did you dream?"

"Why Wednesday night I dreamt that you was sitting over there by the bed, and Sid and Mary and Joe Harper's mother was sitting here with you."

"Why, that's true! Did you dream anything else?"

"Just let me think a moment. Oh, yes. You said I warn't bad, only mischievous."

"And then you began to cry."

"So I did. So I did."

"Well, goodness gracious! I did say that! Go on, Tom!"

"And then you began to cry."

"So I did. So I did."

"Then Mrs. Harper, she began to cry, and said Joe was just the same and she wished she hadn't whipped him for taking cream when she'd throwed it out her own self."

"Tom! The spirit was upon you! You was a-prophesying[1]—that's what you was doing! Land alive, go on, Tom!"

"Then Sid said he hoped I was better off where I was gone to, but if I'd been better sometimes . . . And you shut him up sharp," Tom added.

"I surely did!"

"And Mrs. Harper told about Joe scaring her with a fire-cracker, and you told about Peter and the Pain-Killer—"

[1] a-prophesying—able to see things that he didn't witness in person.

"Just as true as I live!"

"And then there was a whole lot of talk 'bout searching the river for us, and 'bout having the funeral Sunday, and then you and old Miss Harper hugged and cried, and she went home."

"It happened just so, as sure as I'm a-sitting here. Tom you couldn't have told it better if you'd a seen it! And then what?"

"Then you prayed for me and you went to bed and I was so sorry that I wrote on a piece of bark: 'We ain't dead—we're only off being pirates.' And I put it on the table by the candle. Then I kissed you on the lips."

"Did you, Tom, did you! I just forgive you everything for that!" And she grabbed the boy in a crushing hug that made him feel like a terrible liar.

"It was very kind, even though it was only a dream," Sid said in a quiet voice.

"Shut up, Sid!" said Aunt Polly. "A body does just the same in a dream as he'd do if he was awake. Here's a big apple I've been saving for you Tom, if you was ever found again. Now go along to school. I have so much to think about, and just wait 'til I tell Mrs. Harper!"

The children left for school, and the old lady went to call on Mrs. Harper to tell her about Tom's marvelous dream.

What a hero Tom was now! He did not go skip-
ping and dancing, but moved in a **swagger**,[2] like a
pirate who knew the public eye was on him. And it
surely was. Smaller boys followed along after him,
proud to be seen in his company.

At school, the children made so much of him and
Joe that the two heroes became terribly "stuck-up."
They told of their adventures again and again. Then
they pulled out their pipes and began puffing away,
and the children around them almost fainted at
the sight.

Tom decided that he didn't need Becky
Thatcher now. He had **glory**,[3] and that was enough.
Maybe she would want to "make up." Well, let
her—she would see that he could be as cold as
some other people!

Presently Becky arrived. Tom pretended not to
see her. He moved away and joined a group of boys
and girls and began to talk.

Becky began playing, but she was clearly hoping that Tom would speak to her. Then she saw that
Tom was talking more to Amy Lawrence than to
anyone else. She felt a sharp pang and was upset at

---

[2] **swagger**—proud or showy way of walking.

[3] **glory**—great honor and praise given by others.

once. She walked over to the group and said in a loud voice: "Why Mary Austin! I've been looking for you. I wanted to tell you about the picnic."

"O, that's jolly. Who's going to give it?"

Now she was angry and knew what she had to do.

"My ma's going to let me have one. I'm going to have everyone who is friends with me—or wants to be." She glanced at Tom, but he appeared to be busy talking to Amy Lawrence.

Becky's lips turned down and the tears came to her eyes. Now she was angry and knew what she had to do.

At recess, Tom continued flirting with Amy. He looked to see if Becky noticed, but saw to his **dismay**[4] that she was talking to Alfred Temple, a new boy. Becky was sitting on a little bench with Alfred and was reading aloud from a book. All of a sudden, Tom hated himself for throwing away the chance Becky had offered him. He called himself a fool and all the hard names he could think of.

Tom ran home at noon. He could not bear Amy's happy chatting for another second, and could not stand the sight of Becky and Alfred

---

[4] **dismay**—great worry.

together. Becky began looking at the book again with Alfred, but when she saw that Tom was not there to watch, she lost interest. Poor Alfred, seeing that he was losing her, kept exclaiming: "Oh here's a jolly picture! Look at this!" Becky lost patience at last and said: "Oh, don't bother me! I don't care for the book!" and burst into tears. Then she got up and walked away.

Alfred ran alongside her and tried to comfort her, but she said: "Go away and leave me alone, can't you? I hate you!"

Before she was halfway home, however, Becky had stopped crying. She decided to stay angry with Tom. She didn't care a bit. She would hate Tom Sawyer forever.

CHAPTER EIGHTEEN

The Cruelty of "I Didn't Think"

Aunt Polly is angry with Tom because he lied to her about the dream. She's also hurt by his cold heart.

Tom arrived at home in a terrible mood. But the first thing his aunt said showed him that he had come to the wrong place for sympathy.

"Tom, I'd like to skin you alive!"

"Auntie, what have I done?"

"Well, you've done enough. I went over to Sereny Harper's, like an old softy, expecting that she's going to be excited about that fool dream you told me. And then what do you know, she said she'd found out from Joe that you had snuck over here that night from the island and heard all the talk we had. I'll tell you, Tom, it makes me feel so bad to think you could let me go to Mrs. Harper and make such a fool of myself."

Here was something new. This morning, the story about the dream had seemed like a good joke. Now it just looked mean and **shabby**.[1] Tom hung

> **"Auntie, I wish I hadn't done it—but I didn't think."**

his head and said: "Auntie, I wish I hadn't done it— but I didn't think."

"O, child you never think. You never think of anything but your own self. You came all the way over here from Jackson's Island in the night to laugh at our troubles, but you couldn't be bothered to pity us and save us from sorrow."

"Auntie, I know now it was mean, but I didn't mean to be mean. I didn't, honest. And besides I didn't come over here to laugh at you that night."

"What did you come for, then?"

"It was to tell you not to be worried about us, because we hadn't got drownded."

"Tom, Tom, I would be the thankfullest soul in this world if I could believe you, but I know it's not the truth."

---

[1] **shabby**—hateful.

"But it is true, Auntie! That's why I came that night."

"O, Tom, don't lie—don't do it. It only makes things a hundred times worse."

"It ain't a lie, Auntie, it's the truth. I wanted to keep you from feeling sad—that was why I came."

"I'd give the whole world to believe you, Tom, but the story makes no sense. Why didn't you tell me if that's what you wanted to do?"

"Why, you see, Auntie, when you started talking about the funeral, I had the idea of our coming and hiding in the church, and I somehow couldn't bear to spoil it. So I put the bark in my jacket pocket and kept mum."

"What bark?"

"The bark I wrote on to tell you we'd gone pirating. Now I wish you'd waked up when I kissed you—I do, honest."

The hard lines in his aunt's face relaxed, and a sudden tenderness dawned in her eyes. "Did you kiss me, Tom?"

"Why, yes, I did."

"Are you sure you did, Tom?"

"Why yes I did, Auntie—certain sure."

"What did you kiss me for, Tom?"

"Because I loved you so, and you laid there moaning, and I was so sorry."

The words sounded like truth. The old lady's voice was shaking when she said: "Kiss me again, Tom! And then be off with you to school, now, and don't bother me anymore."

The moment he was gone, she ran to a closet and got out the filthy jacket that Tom had taken with him to Jackson's Island. Then she stopped herself and said: "No, I don't dare

Twice she put out her hand to pick up the jacket again, and twice she stopped herself.

look. Poor boy, I reckon he's lied about the bark too. But it's a blessed, blessed lie, and it's given me such comfort. I don't want to know if it's a lie. I won't look."

She put the jacket away, and stood thinking a minute. Twice she put out her hand to pick up the jacket again, and twice she stopped herself. Then she gave up and stuck her hand in the pocket. A moment later, she was reading Tom's piece of bark through her tears and she was saying: "I could forgive the boy, now, for a million sins!"

CHAPTER NINETEEN

Tom Takes Becky's Punishment

Back in school, Tom says he's sorry to Becky, but she still won't speak to him. He figures out a way to earn her favor again.

There was something about Aunt Polly's behavior, when she kissed Tom, that swept away his bad mood and made him feel happy again. He headed back toward school and had the luck of coming upon Becky Thatcher at the top of Meadow Lane. Without stopping to think, he ran to her and said: "I acted mighty mean today, Becky, and I'm so sorry. I won't ever, ever do it again. Please make up, won't you?"

The girl stopped and looked at him **scornfully**.[1] She said: "I'll thank you to keep yourself to yourself, Mr. Thomas Sawyer. I'll never speak to you again."

She tossed her head and walked by. Tom was so stunned that he could not say a word. But he was angry anyway. He walked slowly back into the schoolyard, all the while wishing Becky were a boy so that he could fight her for real. In a little bit, Tom saw Becky again and said something mean to her. She said something just as mean back again, and now they were both very angry.

Poor girl, she did not know how fast she was nearing trouble. The teacher, Mr. Dobbins, had reached middle age with an **unfulfilled**[2] dream. He had always wanted to be a doctor, but had ended up being the village schoolmaster. Every day he took a secret book out of his desk and read it when the children were busy with their studies. He kept the book locked in his desk. The children were curious about the book.

Now, as Becky was passing by Mr. Dobbins's desk, she noticed that the key was in the lock! It was

---

[1] **scornfully**—angrily.
[2] **unfulfilled**—unsatisfied.

a wonderful moment. She glanced around, found herself alone, and opened the drawer. In the next minute, she had the book in her hands. The title page, which said "Professor somebody's Anatomy" told her nothing, so she began to turn the pages. She came upon a drawing of a human figure that was completely naked. At that moment a shadow fell on the page and Tom Sawyer stepped in the room and caught a glimpse of the picture. Becky slammed the book shut at once, but in the process ripped a page halfway down the middle. She thrust the book back into the desk and turned the key. Then she burst into tears.

"Tom Sawyer, you are just as mean as you can be, to sneak up on a person like that!" she sobbed.

"I wasn't sneaking anywhere!"

"You ought to be ashamed of yourself, Tom Sawyer. You know you're going to tell on me, and O, what shall I do, what shall I do! I'll be whipped, and I never was whipped in school."

Tom stood still, a little confused. Then he said to himself: "What a strange kind of fool a girl is. Well, of course I ain't going to tell old Dobbins on this little fool. There's other ways of getting even

> "You know you're going to tell on me, and O, what shall I do, what shall I do!"

with her that ain't so mean. But Becky's in trouble now. Old Dobbins will figure out she did it. Her face will give her away for sure."

Tom shot a glance at Becky and saw that she looked like a scared and helpless rabbit.

Soon the other children came back into the school. Tom couldn't concentrate on his studies because he was worried about Becky. He didn't want to feel sorry for her, but he couldn't help it.

A whole hour went by. Mr. Dobbins sat at his desk, watching the children study. By and by, he straightened himself up, yawned, and then unlocked his desk. He took out his book and prepared to read. Tom shot a glance at Becky and saw that she looked like a scared and helpless rabbit.

The next moment, the red-faced teacher faced the school and said: "Who tore this book?"

There was not a sound. One could have heard a pin drop. Mr. Dobbins searched face after face for signs of guilt.

"Benjamin Rogers, did you tear this book?" A **denial.**[3] Another pause.

"Joseph Harper, did you?"

---

[3] **denial**—saying that he didn't.

Another denial. Tom grew more and more nervous. The master looked over the group of boys and then turned to the girls.

"Amy Lawrence?"

A shake of the head.

"Gracie Miller?"

No again. The next girl was Becky Thatcher. Tom was shaking from head to foot with nervousness.

"Rebecca Thatcher," (Tom glanced at her face— it was white with terror)—"did you tear this book?"

A thought shot like lightning through Tom's brain. In an instant, he sprang to his feet and shouted—"*I* done it!"

Everyone looked at him in surprise. Tom stood still for a moment and then walked forward to receive his punishment. As he moved, he saw the gratitude in Becky's eyes. That seemed pay enough for a hundred whippings! Tom was overjoyed.

CHAPTER TWENTY

Huck Finn Quotes
from the Bible

Summer break has finally arrived. Tom comes down with the measles. When he is able to get out of bed again, he discovers that the whole town has "found" religion.

Summer vacation came at last. At first, Tom enjoyed his freedom. But soon enough, time began to hang heavy on his hands. He tried to write in a diary, but nothing happened for three days, so he forgot about it.

The Fourth of July was a failure since it rained. A circus came. The boys played circus for three days afterward in tents made of rags. Then that game grew old. A phrenologist[1] and a mesmerizer[2]

---

[1] phrenologist—person who predicts the future based on the shape and bumps on a person's head.

[2] mesmerizer—hypnotist.

came and went—leaving the village duller than before.

There were some boys-and-girls' parties, but they were few and far between. Besides, Becky Thatcher was gone to her Constantinople home to stay with her parents during vacation, so there was no bright side to life anywhere.

For two long weeks, Tom lay a prisoner in his bed.

Of course, the terrible secret of the murder was a constant misery to Tom. He thought about it as little as he could. Then came the measles.

For two long weeks, Tom lay a prisoner in his bed. He was very ill and interested in nothing. When he got up on his feet at last and moved slowly into the village square, he found that a sad change had come over everything and every creature. There had been a **"revival,"**[3] and everybody had "got religion"—even the boys and girls. Tom went walking about, hoping against hope for the sight of one sinful face, but he couldn't find a single one. He found Joe Harper reading the Bible and Ben Rogers visiting the poor with a basket of religious books. In desperation, he ran to find

---

[3] **revival**—large religious meeting.

Huckleberry Finn. When Huck recited Scripture[4] to him, however, Tom's heart broke and he crept home and back to bed. He began to worry that he was the only person in the village who would not be saved.[5]

Later that night, a terrible storm came. There was hard rain, awful claps of thunder, and blinding sheets of lightning. Tom covered his head with the sheets and waited to die. He assumed that the storm had been sent to teach him a lesson about being sinful.

Soon the storm ended, without killing Tom. His first thought was to be grateful and to **reform**.[6] His second thought was to wait—for there might not be any more storms.

The next day the doctor was back. Tom had had a **relapse**.[7] The three weeks he spent on his back this time seemed like forever. When he got up again, however, the town seemed back to normal. He found Jim Hollis acting as judge in a court that was trying a cat for the murder of a bird. He found Joe Harper and Huck Finn up an alley eating a stolen melon. Poor lads! They—like Tom—had suffered a relapse.

---

[4] Scripture—passages from the Bible.
[5] be saved—go to Heaven after dying.
[6] **reform**—change for the better.
[7] **relapse**—turn for the worse.

CHAPTER TWENTY-ONE

Muff Potter Is Saved

Muff Potter's murder trial begins. Tom and Huck are
overcome with guilt. At the trial, Tom is called as a witness.
Injun Joe escapes.

At last the sleepy town woke up a bit. It was time for
Muff Potter's murder trial. Once again, the murder
became the most important topic of the village. Tom
could not get away from it. Every word about the
murder went straight to his heart, for his conscience
was still very bothered. He took Huck to a lonely
place to have a talk with him. He figured it might
make them feel better to talk things over. Also, he
wanted to be sure that Huck had kept the secret.

"Huck, have you ever told anybody about—that?"

"'Bout what?"

"You know what."

"O—'course I haven't, Tom."

"Never a word?"

"Never a single word, so help me. What makes you ask?"

"Well, I was afeard."

"Why Tom Sawyer, we wouldn't be alive two days if word got out. You know that."

> "I reckon we're safe as long as we keep quiet."

Tom felt more comfortable. "Well, that's all right, then. I reckon we're safe as long as we keep quiet. But let's swear again, anyway. It's more surer."

"I'm agreed."

So they swore again.

"I'll tell you, Huck, that all this talk about Muff Potter makes me shiver."

"Me too," observed Huck. "Muff ain't a bad man, that's the thing. He ain't never done anything to hurt anybody. He just fishes a little, to get money to get drunk on. But he's kind of good. He gave me half a fish, once, when there warn't enough for two, and lots of times he kind of stood by me when I was out of luck."

"Well, he fixed kites for me, Huck, and tied hooks onto my fishing line. I wish we could get him out of there."

"My! We couldn't get him out Tom. And besides, it wouldn't do any good. They'd just ketch him again."

"Yes—so they would. But I hate to hear 'em talk about him so mean-like when he never done nothing."

"I do too, Tom. Lord, I hear 'em say he's the bloodiest-looking murderer in this country."

"Yes, they talk like that all the time. I've heard 'em say that if he was to get free, they'd **lynch**[1] him."

"And they'd do it, too."

The boys had a long talk, but it brought them little comfort. As evening fell, they found themselves hanging around the little jail. The boys did as they had often done before. They went to the prison window and gave Potter some tobacco and matches. He was on the ground floor, and there were no guards.

Muff's thanks for their gifts had always made Huck and Tom feel terrible. They felt like **cowards**[2] when Potter said:

"You've been mighty good to me, boys—better than anybody else in this town. Sometimes I says to myself: 'I used to mend all the boys' kites, and

---

[1] **lynch**—hang. A lynching is a deadly punishment done by a mob without a trial.

[2] **cowards**—people who have no courage.

show 'em where the good fishin' places was, but now they've all forgot old Muff. All except for Tom and Huck—they don't forget him,' says I.

"Well, boys, I done an awful thing. I was drunk and crazy at the time, and now I got to swing[3] for it, and it's right since I did this terrible thing. But since you've been friendly to me, boys, git up on one another's backs and stick your hands through the bars here so that we can shake hands. That's it. Your hands are little and weak, but they've helped Muff Potter a whole lot, and they'd help him more if they could."

Tom went home very upset, and his dreams that night were full of horrors. The next day and the day after, he hung about the courtroom, but couldn't bring himself to go in. Huck was having the same problem. They kept their ears open to hear what was happening in court, but it was always terrible news. Potter was sure to be found guilty.

Tom was out late that second night of the trial, and came to bed through the window. He was terribly excited and barely slept at all that night.

---

[3] swing—die by hanging.

The next morning was the day of the jury's decision. After a long wait, the jury filed in[4] and took their places. Shortly afterwards, Potter, pale and worn out, was brought in. He was all in chains. The guard seated him where all the curious eyes could stare at him, including the **unwavering**[5] eyes of Injun Joe. Another pause, and then the judge arrived and court was in session.

> *The guard seated him where all the curious eyes could stare at him, including the unwavering eyes of Injun Joe.*

A witness was called who testified that he found Muff Potter washing in the river early in the morning after the murder. The next witness said that a knife was found near the body. A third witness swore he had often seen the knife in Potter's possession.

Potter's **attorney**[6] had no questions for any of these witnesses. The audience was annoyed. Did Potter's attorney plan to throw away his client's life without a fight?

More witnesses told about Potter's guilty behavior at the scene of the murder. They too were allowed to leave the stand without being questioned.

---

[4] filed in—entered in a line, single file.

[5] **unwavering**—fixed, not moving.

[6] **attorney**—lawyer.

At last, the **prosecutor**[7] said: "We have presented all the facts of this terrible crime and believe that Muff Potter is guilty of murder. We rest our case here."

A groan escaped from poor Potter. He put his face in his hands and rocked softly back and forth. Potter's attorney stood up and said:

"Your honor, we have just one witness. [Then to the clerk]: "Call Thomas Sawyer!" A surprised look came over every face in the house, including Potter's. All eyes watched Tom as he rose and took his place on the stand. The boy looked badly scared. The questioning began immediately.

> **"Thomas Sawyer, where were you on the seventeenth of June, at about the hour of midnight?"**

"Thomas Sawyer, where were you on the seventeenth of June, at about the hour of midnight?"

Tom glanced at Injun Joe's mean face and he couldn't speak. The audience listened breathlessly, but the words refused to come. After a few moments, however, the boy got a little of his strength back and managed to say:

"In the graveyard!"

---

[7] **prosecutor**—lawyer who brings a case in court against the person on trial.

A **contemptuous**[8] smile appeared on Injun Joe's face.

"Were you anywhere near Hoss Williams's grave?"

"Yes, sir. I was hidden behind the trees that's on the edge of the grave."

Injun Joe gave a barely noticeable jump.

"Did you carry anything there with you?"

Tom hesitated and then said, "Only a—a—dead cat."

There was a ripple of laughter in the audience.

"We will produce the skeleton of that cat. Now my boy, tell us everything that happened. Tell it in your own way, and don't skip anything. Don't be afraid."

Tom began—slowly at first. But as he grew more comfortable, his words came easily. The audience listened to everything he had to say. They were fascinated by his terrible tale. The story reached its **climax**[9] when the boy said—

"—and as the doctor whacked Muff with the board and he fell, Injun Joe jumped up with the knife and—"

Crash! Quick as lightning, Injun Joe sprang for a window, tore through the crowd, and was gone!

---

[8] **contemptuous**—disrespectful and scornful.
[9] **climax**—high point.

CHAPTER TWENTY-TWO

Splendid Days and Scary Nights

Tom and Huck live in terror that Injun Joe will come back to murder them.

Tom was a hero once more. Just like before, he was the darling of the old and the envy of the young. His name even went into print, for the village paper wrote a story about him. There were some that believed he would be President yet, if he escaped hanging.

Tom's days were days of joy and glory, but his nights were seasons of horror. Injun Joe appeared in all his dreams, and always with death in his eye. Nowadays Tom never went out at night, and Huck felt exactly the same way. Tom had told the whole story to the lawyer the night before the great day of the trial, and Huck was sure word would get out that he was involved.

During the day, Muff Potter's gratitude made Tom glad he had spoken. But at night, he wished he had kept his mouth shut. Half the time, Tom was afraid that Injun Joe never would be found. The other half of the time, he was afraid that he would be. He felt sure he never could draw a safe breath again until that man was dead and Tom had seen the body.

CHAPTER TWENTY-THREE

Seeking the Buried Treasure

Tom feels the urge to hunt for buried treasure. He takes Huck along with him. The two begin digging on Cardiff Hill near an old haunted house.

There comes a time in every boy's life when he has a huge desire to go somewhere and dig for hidden treasure. This desire suddenly came upon Tom one day. He went out to find Joe Harper, but couldn't find him. Next he looked for Ben Rogers, but he had gone fishing. Then he came upon Huck Finn the Red-Handed. Huck was willing to come along, just as Tom expected.

"Where'll we dig?" asked Huck.

"O, most anywhere."

"Why, is there treasure hid all around?"

"No indeed there ain't. It's hid in just a few special places, Huck—sometimes on islands, sometimes in rotten chests under the limb of an old dead tree, just where the shadow falls at midnight. But mostly it's hid under the floor in haunted houses."

"Who hides it?"

"Why robbers, of course—who'd you think? Sunday-school superintendents?"

"I don't know. If 'twas mine, I wouldn't hide it. I'd spend the treasure and have a good time."

"So would I. But robbers don't do it that way. They always hide it and leave it there."

"Don't they ever come back for it?"

"No. They think they will, but they don't because they forget where it is or they die. So it lays there a long time and gets rusty. By and by somebody finds an old yellow paper that tells how to find the treasure. The paper has to be studied for about a week because it's mostly signs and pictures and stuff."

"Have you got one of them papers, Tom?"

"No."

"Well, then, how you going to find the treasure?"

"Well, they always bury it under a haunted house, or on an island, or under a dead tree that's got one limb sticking out. Now, we've tried Jackson's

Island a little, and we can try it again sometime. But there's the old haunted house near the Still-House branch of the river. And of course there's lots of dead-limb trees—dead loads of 'em."

"Is it under all of them?"

"How you talk! No!"

"Then how you going to know which one to go for?"

"Well, I don't know. S'pose we tackle that old dead-limb tree on the hill on the other side of Still-House branch?"

> "S'pose we tackle that old dead-limb tree on the hill on the other side of Still-House branch?"

So they got a **pick**[1] and a shovel and set out on their three-mile walk to Still-House branch. They arrived hot and sweaty, and threw themselves down in the shade of a tree to rest and have a smoke.

"I like this," said Tom.

"So do I."

After they had rested, the boys got down to business and began digging. They worked for half an hour. No result. They **toiled**[2] another half-hour. Still no result. Huck said: "Do they always bury it as deep as this?"

---

[1] **pick**—pickax, a sharp pointed tool used for breaking rocks or hard soil.
[2] **toiled**—worked hard.

"Sometimes—not always. Not usually. I reckon we haven't got the right place."

So they chose a new spot and began digging again. The work dragged a little, but still they made progress. They shoveled away in silence for some time.

> **"Blame it, we must be in the wrong place again. What do you think?"**

Finally Huck leaned on his shovel, wiped his forehead with his sleeve, and said: "Blame it, we must be in the wrong place again. What do you think?"

"Oh, Huck, I know what the matter is! What a bunch of fools we are! You got to find out where the shadow of the limb falls at midnight, and that's where you dig!"

"Then consound it,[3] we've done all this work for nothing. Now hang it all, we got to come back in the night. It's an awful long way. Can you get out?" Huck asked.

"You bet I will," Tom replied. "We've got to do it tonight, too. If somebody sees these holes, they'll know in a minute what's here and they'll go for the treasure."

"Well, I'll come around and meow tonight."

"All right. Let's hide the tools in the bushes."

---

[3] consound it—darn it.

The boys were there that night at the chosen time. They sat in the shadow waiting. It was a lonely place and quiet as could be. Spirits whispered in the rustling leaves, and ghosts lurked in the shadows. The boys were nervous, so they talked little. By and by, they judged that midnight had come. They marked where the shadow fell and began to dig. Their hopes began to rise. Their interest grew stronger, and they dug like mad. The hole deepened and deepened, but they found nothing. At last Tom said, "It ain't any use, Huck, we're wrong again."

"Well, but we can't be wrong. We spotted the shadow to a dot."

"I know it, but then there's another thing."

"What's that?"

"Why, we only guessed at the time. Maybe it was too late or too early."

Huck dropped his shovel. "That's it," said he. "That's the very trouble. We got to give this one up. Besides, this digging is too awful, what with witches and ghosts a-fluttering around so. I feel as if something's behind me all the time, and I'm afraid to turn around. I've been creeping all over, ever since I got here."

"Well, me too, Huck."

"Say, Tom, let's give this place up and try somewhere else."

"All right, I reckon we better."

"Where should we go?"

Tom considered a while and then said, "The haunted house. That's it!"

"Blame it, I don't like haunted houses, Tom. Why they're worse than dead people. Dead people might talk, maybe, but they don't come sliding around in a **shroud**[4] when you ain't noticing and peep over your shoulder the way a ghost does. I couldn't stand something like that, Tom—nobody could."

"All right, Huck, we'll dig there in the daytime."

"Well all right. We'll go to the haunted house if you say so, but I reckon it's taking chances."

They had started down the hill by this time. There in the middle of the moonlit valley below them stood the "haunted" house. It was completely **isolated**,[5] with rotten weeds growing all over the doorsteps. The chimney was all crumbled, and a corner of the roof had caved in.

The boys looked a while, half expecting to see a ghost fly past a window. Then they walked off again and took their way homeward through the woods on the rear side of Cardiff Hill.

---

[4] **shroud**—cloth used to wrap a dead body for burial.

[5] **isolated**—alone.

CHAPTER TWENTY-FOUR

Real Robbers Grab the Box of Gold

The boys continue their treasure hunt. They begin poking around in the haunted house. Suddenly, they are interrupted by the voices of two men.

Around noon the next day, the boys arrived at the dead tree to pick up their tools. Tom was impatient to go to the haunted house. Huck was eager, also, but suddenly said: "Looky-here, Tom, do you know what day it is?"

Tom mentally ran over the days of the week and then quickly lifted his eyes with a startled look in them. He said: "My! It's Friday! I never once thought of it! Blame it, a body can't be too careful,

Huck. We might've got into an awful mess, tackling such a thing on a Friday."

"That's the truth! There's some lucky days, maybe, but Friday ain't one of 'em."

"I'm agreed."

So the boys played Robin Hood all afternoon. As the sun began to sink into the west, they took their way homeward among the long shadows of the trees.

On Saturday, shortly after noon, the boys were at the dead tree again. They had a smoke and a chat in the shade, and then started walking. When they reached the haunted house, there was something so weird and **grisly**[1] about the dead silence. Something was so depressing about the loneliness of the place, that they were afraid, for a moment, to go inside. Then they crept up to the door and took a little peep. They saw a weed-grown, floorless room, an old fireplace, empty windows, a ruined staircase, and cobwebs everywhere. They entered slowly, talking in whispers. They kept their ears open to any sound and were ready to run in an instant.

In a little while, they were able to relax and begin their search of the house. Eventually they

---

[1] **grisly**—horrifying.

threw their tools into a corner and made their way up the stairs. There they found the same signs of **decay**.[2] In one corner they saw a closet that looked sort of mysterious, but it was empty. They were about to go down and begin their work when—

"Shh!" said Tom.

"What is it?" whispered Huck, pulling back in fright.

"Shh!—There!—Hear it?"

"Yes! Oh, my! Let's run!"

"Keep still! Don't you budge! They're coming right toward the door."

The boys stretched themselves upon the floor with their eyes to **knotholes**[3] in the wood.

"They've stopped—No—they're coming! Here they are. Don't whisper another word, Huck. My goodness, I wish I was out of this!"

Two men entered. Each boy said to himself: "There's the old deaf and dumb **Spaniard**[4] that's been around town lately. Never saw the other man before."

The other man was a ragged, **unkempt**[5] creature, with nothing very pleasant in his face. The Spaniard

---

[2] **decay**—rot.

[3] **knotholes**—holes where sections have dropped out of a piece of wood.

[4] deaf and dumb Spaniard—Spanish person who cannot hear or talk.

[5] **unkempt**—messy and unclean.

was wrapped in a serape.[6] He had a messy white beard and long, white hair that flowed from under his sombrero.[7] He also wore green glasses. The men sat down on the ground, facing the door, with their backs to the wall. The man the boys didn't recognize began speaking

The man's voice made the boys gasp and shake.

"I've thought it all over," said he, "and I don't like it. It's dangerous."

"Dangerous!" grunted the "deaf and dumb" Spaniard—to the huge surprise of the boys. "That's ridiculous!"

The man's voice made the boys gasp and shake. It was Injun Joe's! There was silence for some time. Then Joe said: "What's more dangerous than that job we did up yonder? But nothing came of that."

"That's different. That was a ways up the river, and there wasn't another house around. I tell you, I want to leave this house and not come back. Didn't you see those **rascally**[8] boys playing on the hill yesterday?"

The "rascally" boys shivered when they heard this remark and thought how lucky it was that they

---

[6] serape—Latin American colorful woolen cloak.

[7] sombrero—Mexican wide-brimmed hat.

[8] **rascally**—playfully misbehaving.

had remembered it was Friday and had decided not to dig. They wished in their hearts they had waited a year.

The two men got out some food and made lunch. After a long and thoughtful silence, Injun Joe said: "Look here, partner—you go back up the river where you belong. Wait there till you hear from me. I'll take the chance of dropping into town just once more for a look around. We'll do that 'dangerous' job after I've checked things out. Then we're off for Texas! We'll go together!"

This was satisfactory. Both men presently started yawning, and Injun Joe said: "I'm dead for sleep! It's your turn to watch."

He curled down in the weeds and soon began to snore. His partner kicked him once or twice, and he became quiet. Presently the watcher began to nod and his head drooped lower and lower. Soon both men began to snore.

The boys drew a long, grateful breath. Tom whispered: "Now's our chance—come on!"

Huck said: "I can't—I'd die if they was to wake."

Tom begged, but Huck held back. At last Tom rose slowly and softly and started out alone. But the first step he took made such a terrible creak that he sank down almost dead with fright. He never made a second try. The boys lay there counting the dragging minutes. At last they noticed that the sun was setting.

Now one snore stopped. Injun Joe sat up, stared around, and smiled grimly upon his sleeping companion. He kicked the man in the leg and said: "Here! What kind of watchman are you?"

"My! Have I been asleep?"

"Oh, partly, partly. It's nearly time for us to be moving, partner. What'll we do with the loot we've got left?"

"I don't know—leave it here as we've always done, I reckon. No taking it until we start for Texas. Six hundred and fifty in silver's a lot to carry."

"Well, all right. It won't matter if we have to come back here once more. But let's bury it, just to be safe."

"Good idea," said Joe's partner, who walked across the room, knelt down, and pulled up one of the stones from the fireplace **hearth**.[9] From the hole he yanked out a bag that jingled pleasantly. He subtracted from it twenty or thirty dollars for himself

---

[9] **hearth**—stone, concrete, or brick area where nothing can burn.

and as much for Injun Joe and then passed the bag to Joe, who was on his knees in the corner digging furiously with his knife.

The boys forgot their fears and worries in an instant. With happy eyes they watched every movement. This was luck! Six hundred dollars was

They would know exactly where to dig!

money enough to make half a dozen boys rich! Here was the easiest kind of treasure-hunting in the world. They would know exactly where to dig! They poked each other in their excitement.

Suddenly, Joe's knife struck upon something. "Hello!" said he.

"What is it?" asked the other man.

"It's a box, I believe. Here—give me a hand and we'll see what it's here for. Never mind, I've got it." He reached his hand in, opened up the lid, and said: "Man, it's money!"

The two men examined the handful of coins. They were gold. The boys above were almost as excited as the men.

Joe's companion said: "We'll make quick work of this. There's an old rusty pick over amongst the weeds in the corner by the fireplace. I saw it a minute ago."

He ran and brought the boys' pick and shovel. Injun Joe took the pick, looked at it carefully, shook his head, and then began to use it. Soon they had the whole box out of the hole. It was not very large, but it was filled to the top with coins.

The men looked at the treasure awhile in happy silence.

"Partner, there's thousands of dollars here," said Injun Joe.

"People always said that Murrel's gang[10] hung around here one summer," the stranger observed.

"I know it," said Injun Joe. "I'd guess that this belonged to them."

"Now you won't need to do that job."

Joe frowned and said: "You don't know me, I guess. Robbery ain't the point of that job. It's revenge!" A cruel light shown in his eyes. "I'll need your help on it. When it's finished, then we're off to Texas. Now go home to your Nance and your kids and wait until you hear from me."

"Well—if you say so. What'll we do with this—bury it again?"

---

[10] Murrel's gang—John A. Murrel was a famous robber in the 1840s.

"Yes." [Huge delight overhead.] "No! by the great Sachem,[11] no!" [Huge disappointment overhead.] "I'd nearly forgot. That pick had fresh earth on it!" [The boys were sick with terror in a moment.] "Now I'd like to know how those tools got here. Who brought them here? Have you heard anybody or seen anybody? I'm not going to leave all this money here for someone else to grab. We'll take it to my **den**."[12]

> **"Now I'd like to know how those tools got here. Who brought them here?"**

"Why of course! Might have thought of that before. You mean Den Number One?"

"No—Number Two—under the cross. The other place is no good. It's too common."

"All right. It's nearly dark enough to start."

Injun Joe got up and went about from window to window, carefully peeping out. Presently he said: "Who could have brought those tools here? Do you reckon they can be upstairs?"

The boys stopped breathing. Injun Joe put his hand on his knife, stopped a moment, and then turned toward the stairway. Then he came creaking up the stairs. The terrified boys thought of the

---

[11] "by the great Sachem"—by God.
[12] **den**—hiding place.

closet, but could not move because they were so scared. Suddenly, there was the crash of rotten wood, and Injun Joe landed on the ground in the middle of the ruined stairway. He pulled himself up, cursing all the while. His companion said:

"Now what's the use of doing all that? If it's anybody, and they're up there, let them stay there—who cares? If they want to jump down, now, and get into trouble, who objects? It will be dark in fifteen minutes—and then let them follow us if they want to. I'm willing. In my opinion, whoever brought those things here probably thought we were ghosts or devils or something and took off running long ago."

Joe grumbled a while and then agreed with his friend. Shortly afterward they slipped out of the house and moved toward the river with their precious box.

Tom and Huck rose up, weak with relief. They watched the two men walk away. When they judged it was safe, they jumped down from the second floor and started toward home. They did not talk much, for they were both too busy hating the bad luck that had made them leave the pick and shovel right there in plain sight. If it hadn't been for that, Injun Joe would have hidden the silver and the gold right in front of their eyes. The boys would have been rich!

On their way home, they decided to keep a lookout for the "Spaniard," since he had said that he was going to go back into town one more time. Then they would follow him to "Number Two," wherever that might be. Suddenly, a ghastly thought occurred to Tom:

"Revenge? What if he means us, Huck!"

"Oh, don't say it!" said Huck, nearly fainting.

They talked it all over and decided that he might mean someone else entirely, or maybe just Tom himself, since Tom was the one who had testified.

Tom wasn't exactly comforted by this thought. He would rather have had company if he was going to be in danger for his life!

CHAPTER TWENTY-FIVE

Trembling on
the Trail

*Now that they know there really is some treasure to
hunt for, Tom and Huck begin making careful plans. Tom
believes that Injun Joe may be hiding out in a tavern
room in town.*

Tom dreamt about Saturday's adventures that
night. Four times he had his hands on that rich
treasure, and four times it turned into nothing. In
the early morning light he thought of the adventure. He noticed it seemed strangely far off, as if it
had happened in another life. Then it occurred to
him that the great adventure might have been just
a dream!

As it grew lighter, however, the events of Saturday grew sharper in his memory. He began thinking that it might not have been a dream after all. But how could he find out for sure? He would grab a quick breakfast and go find Huck.

Huck was sitting on the deck of a raft, **listlessly**[1] dangling his feet in the water and looking very upset.

"'It wasn't a dream, then!" Tom cried out. "Somehow I thought it might have been."*

"Hello, Huck!"

"Hello, yourself." [Silence for a minute.] "Tom, if we'd a left the blame tools at the dead tree, we'd have got all that money. O, ain't it awful!"

"'It wasn't a dream, then!" Tom cried out. "Somehow I thought it might have been."

"A dream! It wasn't that, for sure. If them stairs hadn't broke down, you'd have seen for sure that it was no dream."

"Well, then. It's time to find Injun Joe and track down that money!"

"Tom, we'll never find him. Besides, I'd feel mighty shaky if I was to see him again."

"Well, so would I, but I'd like to see him, anyway, and track him down at his Number Two."

---

[1] **listlessly**—quietly, with very little energy.

"Number Two—yes, that's what they said. I been thinking about that. But I can't make nothing of it. What do you reckon it means?"

"I dunno. Say, Huck—maybe it's the number of a house!"

"No, Tom, that ain't it. If it is, it ain't in this one-horse town. There ain't no numbers here."

"Well, that's so. Lemme think a minute. Here— it's the number of a room—in a **tavern**,² you know!"

"Oh, that's an idea! There're only two taverns in town. We can find out quick."

"You stay here, Huck, till I come back."

Tom was off at once. He found that in the nicest tavern in town, No. 2 had long been occupied by a young lawyer, who was still living there.

In the other tavern, which was not so nice, Room No. 2 was more of a mystery. The tavern-keeper's young son said it was kept locked all the time. He said he never saw anybody go into it or come out of it except at night. He also said that he thought the room was haunted, because he had seen a light in there last night.

"That's what I've found out, Huck. I reckon that's the very No. 2 we're after."

---

² **tavern**—bar with rooms for rent.

"I reckon it is, Tom. Now what you going to do?"

"Lemme think."

Tom thought a long time. Then he said: "I'll tell you. The back door of No. 2 comes out into an alley that's between the tavern and that old brick store. Now, you get hold of all the door-keys you can find, and I'll do the same. When it gets dark tonight, we'll go over there and try all of 'em. Mind, though, that you keep a lookout for Injun Joe. He said he was going to drop into town and spy around a little. Remember? If you see him, just follow him. If he don't go to that No. 2, then that ain't the place where the treasure is hid."

"Lordy, I don't want to follow him by myself!"

"Why, it'll be night, though. He wouldn't have to see you."

"Well, I reckon that's true. I'll try to track him. I will, by jingo!"

"Now you're talking! Don't you ever weaken, Huck, and I won't."

CHAPTER TWENTY-SIX

Injun Joe and Room No. 2

*Tom makes his way into Room No. 2 and finds Injun Joe
there, drunk and fast asleep. The boys decide to keep an
eye on No. 2 from now on.*

That night, Tom and Huck were ready for their
adventure. They hung around near the tavern until
after nine. Each kept a careful lookout. Nobody
entered the alley or left it, and nobody who looked
like a Spaniard entered or left the tavern door.
Because the night was cloudless and the moon
bright, they decided to wait and try the keys the
next night.

On Tuesday, the boys had the same bad luck.
Also Wednesday. But Thursday night was much

cloudier. Tom slipped out with his aunt's old tin lantern and a large towel to cover it with. He hid the lantern along the way, and the watch began. An hour before midnight, the tavern closed up and its lights were put out. No Spaniard had been seen. Nobody had entered or left the alley. Everything was quiet.

It seemed hours since Tom had disappeared! Surely he must have fainted, or maybe he was dead.

After midnight, Tom got his lantern, lit it, and the two adventurers crept in the darkness toward the tavern. Huck stood watch, and Tom felt his way into the alley. Huck waited and waited. It seemed hours since Tom had disappeared! Surely he must have fainted, or maybe he was dead. Maybe his heart had burst under terror and excitement! In his nervousness, Huck moved closer and closer to the alley. Suddenly there was a flash of light, and Tom came tearing by.

"Run!" screamed Tom. "Run for your life!"

He didn't need to repeat it, of course. Once was enough for Huck. The two boys ran like crazy until they reached the shed of a deserted slaughter-house[1] at the other end of the village. Just as soon as they

---

[1] slaughter-house—place where animals are killed for food.

got inside the door, the storm burst, and the rain poured down. When Tom got his breath, he said:

"Huck, it was awful! I tried two of the keys, just as soft as I could, but they seemed to make such a racket that I could hardly take a breath. They wouldn't turn the lock, either. Well, without noticing what I was doing, I took hold of the knob, and open comes the door! It warn't locked! I hopped in, pulled the towel off the lantern, and great Caesar's ghost!"

"What!—What'd you see, Tom!"

"Huck, I most stepped onto Injun Joe's hand!"

"No!"

"Yes! He was laying there, sound asleep on the floor, with his old patch on his eye and his arms spread out."

"Lordy, what did you do? Did he wake up?"

"No, he never moved. Drunk, I reckon. I just grabbed that towel and started running!"

"I'd never have remembered the towel, I bet!"

"Well, I did. My aunt would've made me mighty sick if I had lost it."

"Say, Tom, did you see that box?"

"Huck, I didn't wait to look around. I didn't see the box, and I didn't see the cross. I didn't see anything but a bottle and a tin cup on the floor by Injun Joe. Oh yes, and I saw two barrels and lots more bottles in the room. Huck, the room was full of whisky!"

There was a long pause. Then Tom continued: "Looky-here, Huck, let's not try to go into No. 2 until we know Injun Joe's not in there. It's too scary. Now if we watch every night, we'll be dead sure to see him go out sometime or another. Then we'll go in and snatch that box quicker than lightning!"

> **"Now if we watch every night, we'll be dead sure to see him go out sometime or another."**

"Well, I'm agreed. I'll watch the whole night long, and I'll do it every night, too, if you'll do the other part of the job."

"All right, I will. You come meow for me if you see him going anywhere."

"Agreed!" Huck said with excitement.

CHAPTER TWENTY-SEVEN

Huck Saves the Widow

Becky invites a group of boys and girls on a picnic. The children explore a nearby cave. In town, Huck watches as Injun Joe and a companion leave Room No. 2 with a box. He follows them and overhears a horrible plan.

The first thing Tom heard on Friday morning was a happy piece of news. Judge Thatcher's family had come back to town the night before. Tom forgot about Injun Joe and the treasure for a moment and began thinking again about Becky. He ran over to her house, and they had a wonderful time playing "I-Spy" and other games with a crowd of their schoolmates. Becky begged her mother to say that the next day would be fine for the long-promised and long-delayed picnic. Finally Mrs. Thatcher agreed.

Becky's delight was huge and so was Tom's. The invitations were sent out before sunset, and straightway the young folks of the village were thrown into a fever of preparation. Because he was excited, Tom stayed awake quite late, and was able to listen for Huck's meow. But he was disappointed. No signal came that night.

Morning came at last. By ten or eleven o'clock, a group of happy children had gathered at Judge Thatcher's house, and everything was ready for the picnic. Becky's parents would not be coming with the group, since the children were old enough to look after themselves. The old steam ferryboat was reserved, and the group made their way down the street to the river. Each child was loaded down with a basket of food. Sid was sick and had to miss the fun, so Mary stayed at home to keep him company. The last thing Mrs. Thatcher said to Becky was: "Since you won't get back until late, maybe you should spend the night with one of the girls who lives near the ferry landing, child."

"Then I'll stay with Susy Harper, Mamma."

"Very well. Behave yourself and don't be any trouble."

As they walked along, Tom said to Becky: "Say—I'll tell you what we'll do. Instead of going to Joe Harper's, we'll climb right up the hill and stop at the Widow Douglas's. She'll have ice cream! She has it almost every day—dead loads of it. And she'll be awful glad to have us."

"O, that will be fun!"

Then Becky thought a moment and said: "But what will Mamma say?"

"How'll she ever know?"

The girl turned the idea over in her mind, and said **reluctantly**:[1] "I reckon it's wrong—but—"

"But shucks! Your mother won't know, and so what's the harm? All she wants is for you to be safe, and I bet she'd have said you could go there if you'd have thought of it."

The Widow Douglas's wonderful **hospitality**[2] was so tempting! Becky agreed to come. But they decided to say nothing about their plans to the rest of the group.

Three miles below the town, the ferryboat was waiting. The children jumped onto the boat and steamed across the river. Once they had landed,

---

[1] **reluctantly**—with hesitation.

[2] **hospitality**—welcome and treats for guests.

everyone ran ashore and began romping and playing here and there. After awhile, the group came back to the baskets and began eating. Then they had a quick rest and a chat in the cool shade of the trees. By and by somebody shouted: "Who's ready for the cave?"

Everybody was. Packages of candles were pulled out of the baskets, and the crowd began running up the hill toward the mouth of the cave.

It was said that a person might wander days and nights through the complicated passageways and never find the end of the cave.

The cave had an opening shaped like the letter *A*. Its huge wooden door stood unlocked and unguarded. Inside was a small chamber that was as chilly as an ice-house. The rock walls were dewy with cold sweat. The main passageway of the cave was not more than eight or ten feet wide. This was true for most of the passageways, for McDougal's cave[3] (as it was called) was a huge **labyrinth**[4] of crooked aisles that ran into each other and out again and led nowhere.

It was said that a person might wander days and nights through the complicated passageways

---

[3] This cave, actually called McDowell's cave, is located near Twain's hometown of Hannibal, Missouri.

[4] **labyrinth**—maze or puzzle of passageways.

and never find the end of the cave. That's how large and complex it was. Because of this, no man "knew" the cave. That was an impossible thing. Most of the young men knew a part of it, and it was not usual to go beyond this known part. Tom knew the cave as well as anyone else did.

Together the group moved along the main passageway. About three-quarters of a mile inside the cave, small groups and couples began to break off into separate passageways. By and by, however, one group after another came straggling back to the mouth of the cave. Each child was panting, laughing, and smeared from head to foot with clay from the walls. They were surprised to find that the day had passed and night was coming on fast. The clanging bell of the ferryboat had been calling for half an hour. The children hurried aboard and went sailing merrily away.

Huck was already at his watch when the ferryboat went steaming past the wharf. He heard no noise on board, for the young people were quiet with exhaustion. He wondered what boat it was, and then let it go from his mind and put his attention on the business at hand.

The night was growing cloudy and dark. Ten o'clock came, and the town became quiet. Eleven o'clock came, and the tavern lights were put out. Darkness was everywhere now. Huck waited what seemed a terribly long time, but nothing happened. He was growing impatient. Was there any use? Was there really any use? Why not give it up and go to bed?

No, he would follow them and would trust that he wouldn't be seen in the darkness.

A noise fell upon his ear. He was all attention in an instant. The alley door closed softly. He sprang to the corner of the brick wall. The next moment two men brushed by him, and one seemed to have something under his arm. It must be the box! So they were going to remove the treasure! Why call Tom now? It would be stupid—the men would get away with the box and never be found again. No, he would follow them and would trust that he wouldn't be seen in the darkness. Convinced that this was what he would have to do, Huck stepped out and tiptoed along behind the men, cat-like, with bare feet.

The two men moved up the street three blocks, then turned to the left up a cross street. They went straight ahead, then, until they came to the path that led up Cardiff Hill. They took this path and then began climbing. Huck followed them all the way up the hill, thinking they would stop at any moment.

At one point, he was sure that he had lost them in the bushes. Heavens, what a mess! He listened carefully and then heard the sound of a man clearing his throat not four feet in front of him. Huck's heart shot into his throat, but he swallowed it again. Then he stood there shaking until he thought he would faint. He knew where he was. He knew he was within five steps of the gate leading into the Widow Douglas's grounds. "Very well," he thought. "Let them bury the box there. It won't be hard to find."

Now there was a voice—a very low voice. It was Injun Joe talking: "Damn her, maybe she's got company. The lights are on, even though it's very late."

"I can't see any."

This was that stranger's voice—the stranger they had heard in the haunted house. A deadly chill went to Huck's heart. This, then, was the "revenge" job! His first thought was to run. But then he remembered that the Widow Douglas had been kind to him many times in the past. Maybe these men were going to murder her. If that was the case, he'd have to warn her. But he didn't dare!

Then he heard Injun Joe say: "Yes, she's got company all right."

"Well, then, let's give it up."

"Give it up? You can forget that," growled Injun Joe. "I tell you, I'm not interested in her money. I'm here for revenge. Her husband was rough on me more than once! He was the justice of the peace[5] who jailed me as a vagrant. And that ain't all. It ain't a millionth part of it! He had me horsewhipped[6] in

"Give it up? You can forget that," growled Injun Joe.

front of the jail, right there for everyone to see! I was HORSEWHIPPED!—do you understand? He took advantage of me and died. But I'll take it out on her."

"Oh, don't kill her! Don't do that!"

"Kill? Who said anything about killing? I would kill him if he was here, but I won't kill her. If you want to get revenge on a woman, you don't kill her. Bosh! You go for her looks. You slit her nostrils and you cut her ears open like a pig's."

"By God, that's—"

"Keep your opinion to yourself! It will be safest for you. I'll tie her to the bed. If she bleeds to death, is that my fault? I won't cry if she does. My friend, you'll help me with this for my sake. That's why you're here. I might not be able to do it alone. If you

---

[5] justice of the peace—state judge who rules on small problems.

[6] horsewhipped—beat with a whip used for a horse.

argue, I'll kill you. Do you understand that? And if I have to kill you, I'll kill her—and then I reckon nobody will ever know who done this business."

"Well, if it's got to be done, let's get at it. The quicker the better. I'm all in a shiver."

"Do it now? With company there? No, fool, we'll wait till the lights are out. There's no hurry."

"No, fool, we'll wait till the lights are out. There's no hurry."

Huck wondered if this was his chance. He held his breath and stepped quietly back. He planted his feet carefully and firmly, one after another. Slowly he made his way backwards down the hill and—a twig snapped under his foot! His breath stopped and he listened. There was no sound—the stillness was perfect. With all kinds of relief, he kept moving. He stepped along quickly but cautiously. As soon as he was far enough away, he picked up his **nimble**[7] feet and flew. Down, down he sped, till he reached the house of a Welshman who lived at the bottom of the hill. He banged at the door, and presently the heads of the old man and his two sons poked their way out the windows.

"What's that? Who's banging? What do you want?" the old man demanded.

---

[7] **nimble**—quick.

"Let me in—quick! I'll tell everything."

"Why, who are you?"

"Huckleberry Finn—quick, let me in!"

"Huckleberry Finn, indeed! That ain't a name that will open many doors, that's for sure. But let him in, lads, and let's see what's the trouble."

"Please don't ever tell I told you," were Huck's first words when he got in. "Please don't tell—I'd be killed for sure. But the Widow's been a good friend to me, and I want to tell you—"

"By George, out with it and nobody here'll ever tell, lad."

Three minutes later, the old man and his sons, with their guns, were creeping up the hill. Huck stayed back a bit because he was too afraid to go with them. He hid behind a huge rock and listened quietly. There was an anxious silence, and then all of a sudden there was an explosion of gunfire and a terrible cry.

Huck waited for no particulars.[8] He sprang away and sped down the hill as fast as his legs could carry him.

---

[8] particulars—specific details.

CHAPTER TWENTY-EIGHT

Tom and Becky in the Cave

Huck learns what happened to the Widow Douglas. In the meantime, Aunt Polly and Mrs. Thatcher learn that Becky and Tom have not returned from a visit to the cave.

Right at dawn on Sunday morning, Huck came crawling up the hill and rapped gently at the old Welshman's door. The old men and his boys were asleep but it was not a deep sleep, thanks to the exciting events of the night before. A call came from a window—

"Who's there!"

Huck's scared voice answered in a low tone: "Please let me in! It's only Huck Finn!"

"It's a name that can open this door night or day, lad! Welcome!"

These were strange words to the homeless boy's ears, and the nicest he had ever heard. He could not remember ever hearing the word "Welcome" before. The door was quickly opened and closed again. Huck was given a seat, and the old man and three tall sons gathered around him.

"Now my boy, I hope you're good and hungry, because breakfast will be ready as soon as the sun's up, you can be sure of that! We were hoping you'd come by."

"Well, I was awful scared last night," said Huck, "so I run off. I started running when the pistols went off, and I didn't stop for three miles. I've come now because I wanted to know what happened."

"Well, poor chap, you do look as if you'd had a hard night of it. But there's a bed here for you when you've had your breakfast. Those men, though, they ain't dead, and we're sorry enough for that. You see, we knew right where to put our hands on them, by your description. So we moved along on tip-toe till we got within fifteen feet of them. Just then, I felt a sneeze coming on. It was the worst kind of luck! I tried to keep it back, but it was no use.

"As soon as I sneezed, those rascals went a-running. I sung out, 'Fire, boys!' and blazed away at the place where the rustling was. So did the boys. But they were off in a jiffy, those villains. We ran after them, down through the woods, but never caught them. I judge that our bullets never touched them. They fired a shot each as they started, but their bullets whizzed by and didn't do us any harm. As soon as we lost the sound of their feet, we quit chasing and went down and stirred up the police. I wish we had some sort of description of those fellows. It would help a good deal. Can you describe them, my boy?"

"Oh, please don't tell anybody it was me that told on them! Oh, please!"

"One's the old deaf and dumb Spaniard that's been around here once or twice, and t'other's a mean looking, ragged—"

"That's enough, lad, we know the men! We saw them in the woods behind the Widow's one day, and they ran off. Off with you, boys, and tell the Sheriff. You'll have your breakfast tomorrow morning!"

The Welshman's sons left at once. As they were running out, Huck sprang up and cried: "Oh, please don't tell anybody it was me that told on them! Oh, please!"

"All right, if you say so, Huck, but you should have the credit for what you did."

"Oh, no, no! Please don't tell!"

When the young men were gone, the old Welshman said: "My boy, don't be afraid of me. I wouldn't hurt a hair on your head for all the world. No—I'd protect you—I'd protect you."

Huck looked into the old man's honest eyes a moment. Then he bent over and whispered in his ear: "One of those men—it was Injun Joe!"

The Welshman almost jumped out of his chair. In a moment he said: "Now I think I understand. I knew this had to be the work of a very bad sort of man."

During breakfast the talk went on. The old man explained that the last thing he and his sons had done before going to bed was to get a lantern and examine the fence and the nearby area for marks of blood. They found none, but captured a bulky bundle of—

"Of WHAT?" Huck interrupted quickly. His eyes were staring now, and he held his breath waiting for an answer.

"—of burglar's tools," the old man replied. "Why, what's the matter with you?"

Huck sat back, breathing hard. He was so relieved that the men had not found the treasure! The Welshman eyed him curiously and said—

"Yes, burglar's tools. You seem pretty relieved. What were you thinking we'd found?"

Huck was in a tight place now. He couldn't think of a good answer for the question, so he said sort of **feebly**:[1]

"Sunday-school books, maybe."

The old man laughed out loud. "Poor old chap, you're white as a ghost and exhausted as well. No wonder you're acting a little strange. What you need now is to sleep."

Huck was relieved. Everything seemed to be going fine again. If the men weren't carrying the treasure last night, then it must still be at No. 2. The two villains would be captured later today, and then he and Tom could seize the gold that night without any trouble.

Just as breakfast was ending, there was a knock at the door. Huck jumped for a hiding place. He didn't want anyone to connect him with the events of last night. The Welshman admitted several ladies and gentlemen, including the Widow Douglas. Everyone, it seemed, wanted to hear about last night's excitement.

---

[1] **feebly**—weakly.

The Welshman told the story again and again. The Widow was outspoken in her thanks.

The old man replied: "Don't say a word about it, madam. There's another you need to thank besides me and my boys, but he won't allow me to tell his name. We wouldn't have been there but for him."

Of course this made the whole group extremely curious, but the Welshman would not part with his secret.

> *"Is my Becky going to sleep all day? I figured she would be tired to death."*

There was no Sunday-school during school vacation, but everybody in town came early to church that Sunday to talk about the excitement at the Widow's. News came that the two villains had not yet been captured.

When the sermon was finished, Judge Thatcher's wife dropped alongside of Mrs. Harper as she moved down the aisle with the crowd. She said: "Is my Becky going to sleep all day? I figured she would be tired to death."

"Your Becky?"

"Yes," she answered, with a startled look. "Didn't she stay with you last night?"

"Why, no."

Mrs. Thatcher turned pale and sank into a pew,[2] just as Aunt Polly walked up. Aunt Polly said: "Good morning, Mrs. Thatcher. Good morning, Mrs. Harper. I've got a boy that's turned up missing. I reckon my Tom stayed at your house last night, and now he's afraid to come to church. I need to talk to that boy."

"Joe Harper, have you seen my Tom this morning?"

Mrs. Thatcher shook her head feebly and turned paler than ever. "He didn't stay with us," said Mrs. Harper, beginning to look worried. A look of worry came into Aunt Polly's face.

"Joe Harper, have you seen my Tom this morning?"

"No'm."

"When did you see him last?"

Joe tried to remember, but was not sure he could say. The people had stopped moving out of church. Whispers passed along, and the group started to look uneasy. Children were anxiously questioned. They all said they had not noticed whether Tom and Becky were on board the ferryboat on the homeward trip. It had been dark, and no one

---

[2] pew—church seat.

thought of asking if anyone was missing. One young man finally blurted out his fear that they were still in the cave! Mrs. Thatcher fainted away, and Aunt Polly started to cry.

The alarm swept from lip to lip, from group to group, from street to street, and within five minutes the bells were wildly clanging and the whole town was up! The Cardiff Hill business was forgotten. Horses were saddled, skiffs were readied, and the ferryboat was ordered out. Before the horror was an hour old, two hundred men were pouring down high-road and river toward the cave.

All the long afternoon, the village seemed empty and dead. Many women visited Aunt Polly and Mrs. Thatcher and tried to comfort them. They cried with them, too, and that was better than words. All the long night the town waited for news. When the morning dawned at last, the only word that came was: "Send more candles—and send food." Mrs. Thatcher and Aunt Polly were almost crazed with worry. Judge Thatcher sent messages of hope and encouragement from the cave, but it seemed that nothing could help.

The old Welshman came home toward daylight. He was spattered with candle grease, smeared with clay, and almost worn out. He found Huck still in the bed that had been provided for him. The boy was **delirious**[3] with fever. The doctors were all at the cave, so the Widow Douglas came and took charge of the patient.

Early in the afternoon, parties of discouraged men began to make their way back into the village. The strongest of the citizens continued searching. The only news was that every inch of the cave was going to be thoroughly searched. In one passage-way, far from the section usually seen by tourists, the names "BECKY & TOM" had been found traced upon the rocky wall with candle smoke. Near the words was a dirty bit of ribbon. Mrs. Thatcher recognized the ribbon and cried over it.

Three dreadful days and nights dragged by, and the village sank into a hopeless **stupor**.[4]

---

[3] **delirious**—sick and talking strangely.
[4] **stupor**—daze.

CHAPTER TWENTY-NINE

Found and Lost Again

A terrified Tom and Becky are lost in the cave.

Now to go back to Tom and Becky's share in the picnic. They tripped along the **murky**[1] aisles with the rest of the company, visiting the familiar wonders of the cave. Presently the hide-and-seek game began, and Tom and Becky played along until they grew tired. Then they wandered down a winding passageway. They held their candles up to the walls and read the tangled web-work of names, dates, and sayings that previous visitors had left in years past.

---

[1] **murky**—cloudy and dark.

Still drifting along and talking, they barely noticed that they were now in a part of the cave whose walls were not covered in writing. They used candle-smoke to write their own names on a wall. Then they moved on. Presently they came to a place where a little stream of water trickled over a ledge. Tom squeezed behind the little waterfall and found a steep natural stairway that was between two narrow walls. All at once, the desire to be an explorer seized him.

They wound this way and that, deeper and deeper into the secret depths of the cave.

He called to Becky, who came over and agreed that they should climb the stairs. They made a smoke-mark on the wall for future guidance and started upon their **quest**.[2] They wound this way and that, deeper and deeper into the secret depths of the cave. In one place they found a wide **cavern**[3] with hundreds of **stalactites**[4] hanging from the ceiling. They left the cavern by one of its many other openings and walked near a spring whose bottom was covered with a frost pattern of glittering crystals. At the top of the cave, huge groups of bats

---

[2] **quest**—journey.

[3] **cavern**—very large cave.

[4] **stalactites**—rock formations that grow down from the ceiling of a cave.

packed themselves together—thousands in a bunch. The candlelight disturbed the creatures, and they came flocking down by the hundreds, squeaking and darting at the candles. One of them managed to put out Becky's flame with its wing.

Tom grabbed Becky's hand and pulled her into the first corridor he could find. The bats chased the children a good distance, but they kept running into narrower and narrower passageways. Finally the horrible creatures gave up and went away. Next Tom and Becky came upon an underground lake. Tom wanted to explore its border, but decided it would be best to sit down and rest for a while. Now, for the first time, the deep stillness of the place laid a **clammy**[5] hand upon the spirits of the children. Becky said—

"Why, I didn't notice, but it seems ever so long since I heard any of the others."

"Come to think of it, Becky, we are way down below them. We couldn't hear them here."

Becky grew worried. "I wonder how long we've been down here, Tom. We better start back."

"Yes, I reckon we better."

---

[5] **clammy**—cold and damp.

Chapter Twenty-Nine 189

"Can you find the way, Tom? It's all mixed up to me."

"I reckon I could find it, but we got to think of those bats. If they fly down and snuff out our candles, we'll be in an awful fix. Let's try some other way, so we don't have to go through there."

"Well. But I hope we won't get lost. It would be so awful!" The girl **shuddered**[6] at the thought of it.

They started walking through a corridor, glancing at each new opening to see if there was anything familiar about it. But everything looked new. Tom kept saying in a cheerful voice: "Oh, it's all right. This passageway ain't the one, but we'll come to it right away!"

But he felt less and less hopeful with each failure. Eventually, they began to turn off into different passageways **at random**.[7] They were desperate to find one they recognized. Tom kept saying that it was "all right," but there was such fear in his heart that the words had lost their cheerfulness. Becky clung to his side in fear and tried to keep back her tears. At last she said:

"Oh, Tom, never mind the bats! Let's go back that way! We seem to get worse and worse off all the time."

---

[6] **shuddered**—trembled.

[7] **at random**—without a plan or purpose.

Tom stopped. "Listen!" said he.

Profound[8] silence. It was a silence so deep that even their breathing sounded loud. Tom shouted. The call went echoing down the empty aisles and died out in the distance. It sounded like the ripple of mocking laughter.

"Oh, don't call out again, Tom, it is too horrible," said Becky.

"It is horrible, but I'd better, Becky. They might hear us, you know." He shouted again.

The children stood still and listened, but there was no answering sound. Tom turned and began **backtracking**[9] at once. After a little while, however, he realized that he could not find his way back to the bats.

"Oh, Tom, you didn't make any marks!"

"Becky I was such a fool! Such a fool! I never thought we might want to come back this way! No—I can't find the way. It's all mixed up."

"Tom, Tom, we're lost! We're lost! We'll never get out of this awful place! Oh, why did we ever leave the others!"

---

[8] **Profound**—deep.
[9] **backtracking**—reversing direction.

She sank to the ground and burst into such tears that Tom became worried that she might die, or lose her mind. He sat down next to her and put his arms around her. She buried her face in his chest and she clung to him. Tom begged her to keep up her hope, but she said she could not.

Then he started blaming himself for getting her into this miserable situation. This had a better effect.

Then he started blaming himself for getting her into this miserable situation. This had a better effect. She said that she would try to have hope again. She would get up and follow wherever he might lead if only he would stop talking about himself like that. After all, she said, she was just as much to blame as he was.

So they moved on again, aimlessly. They walked here and there, always looking for a familiar sign. All they could do was to keep moving. By and by, Tom took Becky's candle and blew it out. They would have to save their light. Becky understood, and her hope died again. She knew that Tom had a whole candle and three or four pieces in his pockets—yet he must be very, very careful. It would be terrible to be without light.

A long time after this—they could not tell how long—they came upon a spring. Tom said it was time to rest again. Both were cruelly tired, yet Becky said she thought she could go on a little farther. She was surprised to hear Tom say no. She could not understand it. They sat down, and Tom fastened his candle to the wall in front of them with some clay. Becky said, "Tom, I am so hungry!"

Tom took something out of his pocket. It was a piece of cake from the picnic. "Look at this, Becky," he said, as he divided it in two.

Becky ate with good appetite, while Tom nibbled at his. Afterward, they had as much cold water as they liked. By and by, Becky suggested that they move on again. Tom was silent a moment. Then he said:

"Becky, can you bear it if I tell you something?"

Becky's face paled, but she said she thought she could.

"Well then, Becky, we must stay here, where there's water to drink. That little piece is our last candle!"

Becky started crying again. Tom did what he could to comfort her, but it had little effect. At length Becky cheered a little and said: "Tom! They'll miss us and hunt for us!"

"Yes they will! Certainly they will!"

"Maybe they're hunting for us now, Tom?"

"Why I reckon maybe they are. I hope they are."

"When would they miss us, Tom?"

"When they get back to the boat, I reckon."

"Tom, it might be dark then. Would they notice we hadn't come?"

"I don't know. But anyway, your mother would miss you as soon as they got home."

A frightened look in Becky's face brought Tom to his senses and he saw that he had made a mistake. Becky was not expected home that night! The children became silent and thoughtful. In a moment, a new burst of grief from Becky showed Tom that the thing in his mind had struck hers also. Sunday morning might be half gone before Mrs. Thatcher discovered that Becky was not at Mrs. Harper's.

The children fastened their eyes upon their bit of candle and watched it melt slowly away. They saw the half inch of wick stand alone at last. They watched the feeble flame rise and fall, and then— the horror of complete darkness!

Some time later, the children slept. After what seemed a mighty stretch of time, they awoke to their miseries once more. Tom said it might be Sunday now—or maybe Monday. He tried to get Becky to talk, but her sorrows were too great. All her hopes were gone. Tom said that they must have been missed long ago, and no doubt a search was going on. He would shout, and maybe someone would come. He tried it, but in the darkness the echoes sounded so terrible that he tried it no more.

The hours wasted away, and hunger came again. A portion of Tom's half of the cake was left. They divided that and ate it. But it only made them feel hungrier than before.

By and by, Tom said: "Shh! Did you hear that?"

Both held their breath and listened. There was a sound like the faintest, far-off shout. Instantly Tom answered it, and instantly he and Becky began feeling their way down the corridor in its direction. Presently he listened again, and once more the sound was heard. It seemed a little closer.

"It's them!" said Tom. "They're coming! Come along, Becky—we're all right now!"

The joy of the prisoners was almost **overwhelming**.[10] Their speed was slow, however, because they were afraid of falling. Soon they came

---

[10] **overwhelming**—overpowering.

to a ledge and had to stop. It might have been three feet deep, or it might have been a hundred—there was no way to tell. Tom got down on his chest and reached as far down as he could. No bottom. They would have to stay there and wait until the searchers came. They listened, but the far-off shoutings were growing more distant! In a moment or two more, the sounds were gone altogether. The heart-sinking misery of it! Tom whooped until he was hoarse, but it was of no use. He talked hopefully to Becky, but still they could hear nothing in the darkness.

The children crawled back to the spring. The weary time dragged on. They slept again, and awoke **famished**[11] and heartsick. Tom believed it must be Tuesday by this time.

Now an idea struck him. There were some side passageways near at hand. It would be better to explore some of these than just sit here doing nothing. He took a kite-string from his pocket, tied it to a rock, and he and Becky started off, with Tom in the lead. Tom unwound the string as he felt his way along. At the end of twenty steps the corridor ended in a "jumping-off place." Tom got down on

---

[11] **famished**—very hungry; starving.

his knees and felt below, and then as far around the corner as he could reach. He made an effort to stretch yet a little farther to the right. At that moment, not twenty yards away, a human hand, holding a candle, appeared from behind a rock! Tom lifted up a happy shout, and instantly the hand was followed by the body it belonged to—Injun Joe!

At that moment, not twenty yards away, a human hand, holding a candle, appeared from behind a rock!

Tom was paralyzed. He could not move. To his huge relief, the "Spaniard" turned and ran out of sight. Tom was surprised that Joe had not recognized his voice and come over and killed him for testifying in court. But the echoes must have disguised the sound of it.

Tom's fright weakened every muscle in his body. He said to himself that if he had strength enough to get back to the spring, he would stay there. Nothing would tempt him to run the risk of meeting Injun Joe again. He was careful to keep from Becky what it was he had seen. He told her he had only shouted "for luck."

Eventually, however, hunger and misery overtook fear. Another long wait at the spring and another long sleep brought changes. The children awoke tortured with a raging hunger. Tom thought that it might be Wednesday or Thursday or even Friday. He worried that the searchers might have given up. He decided to explore another passageway. He felt willing to risk Injun Joe and all other terrors. But Becky was very weak. She had given up hope completely. She said she was going to wait now, where she was, and die. She felt it would not be long. She told Tom to go with the kite-line and explore if he chose, but she begged him to come back every once in awhile to speak to her. She also made him promise that when the awful time came for her to die, that he would stay by her and hold her hand until all was over.

Tom kissed her with a choking feeling in his throat. He made a show of confidence, and then took the kite-line in his hand and went **groping**[12] down one of the passageways on his hands and knees. He was overwhelmed with hunger and sick with a feeling of doom.

---

[12] **groping**—feeling about with his hands.

CHAPTER THIRTY

"Turn Out! They're Found!"

The village is heartsick about the children. Then good news arrives.

Tuesday afternoon came and went. It was twilight now, and the village of St. Petersburg still mourned. The lost children had not been found. Public prayers had been offered up for them, but still no good news came from the cave. Most of the searchers had given up the search and had gone back to their daily business, saying that it was plain the children would never be found. Mrs. Thatcher was very ill and out of her mind most of the time. People said it was heartbreaking to hear her call her child's name and then raise her head to listen. Aunt Polly had drooped into a terrible sadness, and her gray hair had grown almost white. The village went to sleep on Tuesday night without much hope.

Away in the middle of the night, a wild peal burst from the village bells. In a moment, the streets were filled with excited people who shouted, "Turn out! Turn out! They're found! They're found!"

The village was completely lit. Nobody went to bed again. It was the greatest night the little town had ever seen. During the first half hour, a line of villagers filed through Judge Thatcher's house. Each person grabbed the saved children and squeezed them and kissed them. People tried to speak, but found they couldn't. They drifted out, raining tears all over the place.

Tom lay upon a sofa with an eager audience around him. He told the history of the wonderful adventure, **exaggerating**[1] a bit here and there to

---

[1] **exaggerating**—overstating.

raise the excitement. He described how he had left Becky and went on an exploring expedition. He told the group how he followed two passageways as far as his kite-line would reach, and then how he followed a third to the fullest stretch of the kite-line. He was about to turn back, he said, when he glimpsed a far-off speck that looked like daylight. He dropped the line and groped toward it. He pushed his head and shoulders through a small hole and saw the broad Mississippi rolling by!

Then he told how he went back for Becky and broke the good news, and she told him not to bother her with such stories, for she was tired and knew she was going to die. He described how he talked and talked and finally convinced her that what he was saying was true. He also told how she almost died for joy when she had groped to where she actually saw the blue speck of daylight, and how they both sat down and cried with gladness after they'd pulled their way out of the hole.

Then he explained that some men came along in a skiff, and he called to them and told them their situation. The men didn't believe the wild story at first, he said, "because," said they, "you are five miles down the river from the opening to the cave." But they took the children aboard, rowed to a house, gave them supper, and made them rest. When it was dark, they brought them home.

Before dawn, Judge Thatcher and the handful of searchers with him were tracked down in the cave and informed of the great news.

Three days and nights of toil and hunger in the cave were not to be shaken off at once, as Tom and Becky soon learned. They stayed in bed all of Wednesday and Thursday, and seemed to grow more and more tired as the days went on. Tom got out of bed a little on Thursday. He was able to go into town on Friday. By Saturday he felt whole again, but Becky did not leave her room until Sunday, and even then she still looked as if she had just finished with a terrible illness.

Tom learned of Huck's sickness and went to see him, but the Widow would not allow him to visit his friend. On Monday he was let in to talk a bit to Huck, but he was warned not to say a word about the adventure in the cave or anything else that might over-excite Huck. The Widow Douglas stayed by to see that he obeyed.

At home Tom learned of the Cardiff Hill event. He also learned that the "ragged man's" body had eventually been found in the river near the ferry landing. It appears that he drowned while trying to escape.

About a week after Tom's rescue from the cave, he started off to visit Huck, who had grown much stronger. Judge Thatcher's house was on Tom's way, so he stopped to see Becky. The Judge and some friends set Tom to talking, and someone asked him in a joking way if he he'd like to go to the cave again. Tom said yes, he thought he wouldn't mind it. The judge said:

"Well, there are others just like you, Tom, I'm sure of that. But we have taken care of that. Nobody will get lost in that cave anymore."

"Why?"

"Because I had its big door repaired and triple-locked. Only I've got the keys."

Tom turned as white as a sheet.

"Why, what's the matter, boy!" the Judge exclaimed. "What is the matter with you, Tom?"

"Oh, Judge, Injun Joe's in the cave!"

CHAPTER THIRTY-ONE

What Happened to Injun Joe

Judge Thatcher, Tom, and some townspeople find Injun Joe's body in the cave. Later, Tom and Huck return to the cave to look for Injun Joe's treasure.

Within a few minutes, the news had spread, and a dozen skiff-loads of men were on their way to McDougal's cave. The ferryboat, loaded with passengers, soon followed. Tom Sawyer was in the skiff that carried Judge Thatcher.

When the cave door was unlocked, a sorrowful sight presented itself. Injun Joe lay stretched upon the ground, dead, with his face close to the crack of the door. It was if he had spent his last moments staring longingly at the light and cheer of the free world outside.

Tom was touched, for he knew by his own experience how this man had suffered. He felt pity, but nevertheless he also felt a great sense of relief and security. He knew that Injun Joe could bother him no more.

Injun Joe's pocket knife lay close by, its blade broken in two. A wooden beam on the bottom of the door had been chipped and cut through. On the other side of the beam lay a huge rock, which the knife could not damage. The only damage done was to the knife itself. But even if there had been no rock there, Injun Joe's labor still would have been useless—he never would have been able to squeeze his body under the door, and he knew it. So he had only hacked at that place in order to be doing something. He wanted to pass the dreary time and give himself something to think about.

Ordinarily one could find half a dozen bits of candle stuck scattered around the inside of the cave. Tourists left them there on their way back outside. But there were none now. The prisoner had searched them out and eaten them. He had also managed to catch a few bats. He had eaten these also, leaving only their claws. The poor man had starved to death.

Injun Joe was buried near the mouth of the cave. The morning after the funeral, Tom took Huck to a private place to have an important talk. By this time, Huck had learned all about Tom's adventure from the Welshman and the Widow Douglas. Tom said he reckoned there was one thing they had not told him. Huck's face saddened. He said:

"Huck, that money wasn't ever in No. 2!"

"I know what you're goin' to tell me. You got into No. 2 and never found anything but whisky. The treasure's gone forever, Tom."

"Huck, that money wasn't ever in No. 2!"

"What!" Huck searched his friend's face carefully. "Tom, have you got on the track of that money again?"

"Huck, it's in the cave!"

Huck's eyes blazed. "Say it again, Tom!"

"The money's in the cave!"

"Tom,—honest injun, now. Are ye tellin' the truth?"

"Yes, I swear it. Will you go in there with me and help get it out?"

"I bet I will! I will if it's where we can blaze our way to it and not get lost."

"Huck, we can do that without the least little bit of trouble in the world."

"Good as wheat! What makes you think the money is—"

"Huck, you just wait till we get in there. I'll show you what I'm talkin' about."

"All right—it's a deal. When do you want to go?"

"Right now, if you say it."

"Let's start right off, Tom."

"All right. We'll want some bread and meat, and our pipes, and a little bag or two. We'll also need two or three kite-strings, and some of these newfangled[1] things they call matches. I tell you many's the time I wished I had a few of those when I was in there before."

Just before noon, the boys borrowed a small skiff from a citizen who was absent and got under way at once. When they were several miles below the cave, they landed.

"Now Huck, where we're a-standing you could touch that hole I got out of with a fishing-pole. See if you can find it."

---

[1] newfangled—recently invented.

Huck searched all the place about and found nothing. Tom proudly marched into a thick clump of bushes and said: "Here it is! Look at it, Huck; it's the most secret hole in this country. You just keep mum about it. All along I've been wanting to be a robber, but I knew I'd have to have a place like this, and I never did. Well, we've got it now, and we'll keep quiet except for Joe Harper and Ben Rogers. They'll be in the gang. There's got to be a gang, you know, or else there wouldn't be any style about it. Tom Sawyer's Gang—it sounds splendid, don't it, Huck?"

"Why it's real bully,[2] Tom. I believe it's better than bein' a pirate."

"Yes, it's better in some ways, because it's close to home and circuses and all that."

By this time everything was ready, and the boys entered the hole, with Tom in the lead. They worked their way to the farther end of the tunnel, and then started letting out their kite strings. A few steps brought them to the spring, and Tom felt a shudder go all through him. He showed Huck the piece of candle-wick perched on a lump of clay against the wall, and described how he and Becky had watched the flame struggle and go out.

---

[2] it's real bully—it's a good idea.

The boys went on and soon entered and followed Tom's other corridor until they reached the "jumping-off place." The candles showed the fact that it was not really a deep hole, but only a steep hill that was perhaps twenty or thirty feet high. Tom whispered: "Now I'll show you something, Huck."

He held his candle up high and said: "Look as far around the corner as you can. Do you see that? There—on the big rock over yonder—done with candle smoke."

"Tom, it's a cross!"

"Now where's your Number Two? 'Under the cross,' hey? Right yonder's where I saw Injun Joe poke up his candle, Huck!"

Huck stared at the cross a while and then said with a shaky voice: "Tom, let's git out of here!"

"What! and leave the treasure?"

"Yes—leave it. Injun Joe's ghost is round about there, certain."

"No it ain't, Huck, no it ain't. It would haunt the place where he died—away out at the mouth of the cave—five miles from here."

The point was well taken. It had its effect. "Tom, I didn't think of that. But that's so. It's luck for us, that cross is. I reckon we'll climb down there and have a hunt for that box."

Tom went first, cutting small steps in the clay hill as he descended. Huck followed. Four avenues opened out of the small cavern in which the great rock stood. The boys examined three of them with no result. They found a small hole in the one nearest the base of the rock. There were a couple of blankets spread down in it. There was also an old belt, some bacon rind, and the well-chewed bones of two or three chickens. But there was no money box. The boys searched and re-searched this place, but it was no use. Tom said:

"I bet you the money is *under* the rock. I'm going to dig in the clay."

"He said under the cross. Well, this comes nearest to being under the cross. It can't be under the rock itself, because that sits solid on the ground."

They searched everywhere once more, and then sat down discouraged. Huck could suggest nothing. By and by Tom said: "Looky-here, Huck, there's footprints and some candle grease on the clay on one side of this rock, but not on the other sides. Now what's that for? I bet you the money *is* under the rock. I'm going to dig in the clay."

"That ain't a bad idea, Tom!" said Huck with enthusiasm.

Tom's pocket knife was out at once, and he had not dug four inches before he struck wood.

"Hey, Huck!—you hear that?"

Huck began to dig and scratch now. Some boards were soon uncovered and removed. They had hidden a natural tunnel that led under the rock. Tom got into the hole and lit his candles as far under the rock as he could, but could see nothing. He said he was going to explore the little tunnel. He crept his way through the narrow passageway, first to the right, then to the left. Huck followed right behind him. Then Tom went around a short curve and exclaimed:

"My goodness, Huck, looky here!"

It was the treasure box, sure enough, sitting in a little cavern, along with an empty powder keg,[3] a couple of guns in leather cases, two or three pairs of old moccasins, a leather belt, and some other rubbish.

"Got it at last!" said Huck, plowing among the old coins with his hand. "My, but we're rich, Tom!"

"Huck, I always reckoned we'd get it. It's just too good to believe, but we *have* got it, sure! Say— let's not fool around here. Let's take it out. Lemme see if I can lift the box."

---

[3] powder keg—small metal barrel used to store gunpowder.

It weighed about fifty pounds. Tom could lift it, but he could not carry it easily.

"I thought so," he said. "They carried it like it was heavy that day at the haunted house. I noticed that. That's why I brought these little bags along."

The money was soon in the bags, and the boys took it up to the cross-rock.

"Now let's fetch the guns and things," said Huck.

"No, Huck—leave them there. They're just what we need when we go to robbing. We'll keep them there. Anyways, it's time to go, Huck. We've been in here a long time. It's getting late, I reckon. I'm hungry, too. We'll eat and smoke when we get to the skiff."

Soon they came out into the clump of bushes, looked carefully around, and found the coast clear. Next, they were lunching and smoking in the skiff. As the sun dipped toward the horizon, they pushed out and got under way. Tom skimmed up the shore through the long twilight, chatting cheerily with Huck, and landed the boat shortly after dark.

"Now Huck," said Tom, "we'll hide the money in the loft of the Widow's wood-shed. I'll come up in the morning and we'll count it and divide it, and then we'll hunt up a place out in the woods for it where it will be safe. You lay quiet here and watch the stuff till I run and grab Benny Taylor's little wagon. I won't be gone a minute."

Tom disappeared, and soon returned with the wagon. They put the two small sacks into it, threw some old rags on top of them, and started off, dragging the load behind them. When the boys reached the Welshman's house, they stopped to rest. Just as they were about to move on, the Welshman stepped out and said:

> "I'll pull the wagon for you. Why, it's not as light as it might be. Got bricks in it?—or old metal?"

"Hallo, who's that?"

"Huck and Tom Sawyer."

"Good! Come along with me, boys! You've kept everybody waiting. Hurry up, trot ahead. I'll pull the wagon for you. Why, it's not as light as it might be. Got bricks in it?—or old metal?"

"Old metal," said Tom.

"I thought so. Hurry along, hurry along!"

The boys wanted to know what the hurry was about.

"Never mind. You'll see, when we get to the Widow Douglas's."

Huck said with some worry—for he was long used to being falsely accused—"Mr. Jones, we haven't done nothing wrong."

The Welshman laughed. "Well, Huck, my boy. Ain't you and the Widow good friends?"

"Yes."

"All right, then. What do you want to be afraid for?"

This question was not completely answered in Huck's slow mind before he found himself pushed, along with Tom, into Mrs. Douglas's living room. Mr. Jones left the wagon near the door and followed.

The place was grandly lighted, and many important people from the village were there. The Thatchers were there, the Harpers, the Rogerses, Aunt Polly, Sid, Mary, the minister, the newspaper editor, and a great many more. Everyone was dressed in their best. The Widow said hello to the boys heartily, and then took them to a bedroom and said: "Now wash and dress yourselves. Here are two new suits of clothes—shirts, socks, everything complete. They're Huck's—no, no thanks necessary, Huck. Mr. Jones bought one and I bought the other. But they'll fit both of you. Get into them. We'll wait for you. Come down when you are slicked up[4] enough."

Then she left.

---

[4] slicked up—cleaned up and dressed up.

CHAPTER THIRTY-TWO

Floods of Gold

The Widow tells Huck that she wants to give him a home and make him respectable. Tom reveals a surprise of his own.

Huck said: "Tom, we can run off, if we can find a rope. The window ain't high from the ground."

"Shucks, what do you want to run off for?"

"Well I ain't used to that kind of a crowd. I can't stand it. I ain't goin' down there, Tom."

"O, bother! It ain't anything. I don't mind it a bit. I'll take care of you."

Sid appeared. "Tom," said he, "Auntie has been waiting for you all the afternoon. Mary got your Sunday clothes ready, and everybody's been worrying. Say, ain't this grease and clay on your clothes?"

"Now Mr. Siddy, you just tend to your own business. What's this party about, anyway?"

"It's one of the Widow's parties that she's always having. This time it's for the Welshman and his sons, on account of that trouble they helped her out of t'other night. And say—I can tell you something, if you want to know."

"He couldn't have his grand secret without Huck, you know!"

"Well, what?"

"Why old Mr. Jones is going to try to spring something on the people here tonight, but I overheard him tell Auntie today about it. It was a secret, but I reckon it's not much of a secret now. Everybody knows—the Widow, too, even though she pretends like she don't. Oh, Mr. Jones was waiting for Huck to get here. He couldn't have his grand secret without Huck, you know!"

"Secret about what, Sid?"

"About Huck tracking the robbers to the Widow's. I reckon Mr. Jones was going to make a big deal over his surprise, but I bet you it will drop pretty flat." Sid chuckled in a very satisfied way.

"Sid, was it you that told?"

"Oh, never mind who it was. Somebody told—that's enough."

"Sid, there's only one person in this town mean enough to do that, and that's you. If you had been in Huck's place, you'd have sneaked down the hill and never told anybody on the robbers. You can't do anything but mean things, and you can't bear to see anybody praised for doing good ones. So there—" and Tom cuffed Sid's ears and helped him to the door with several kicks. "Now go and tell Auntie if you dare. Tomorrow you'll catch it if you do."

Some minutes later, the Widow's guests were at the supper table. At the proper time, Mr. Jones made his little speech. He thanked the Widow for the honor she was doing himself and his sons, but said that there was another person whose modesty—

And so forth and so on. He sprung his secret about Huck's share in the adventure and everybody tried to look surprised. The Widow made a pretty fair show of **astonishment**,[1] and then she heaped so much praise on Huck that he almost forgot the horrible discomfort of his new clothes and the embarrassment of being stared at.

The Widow said she wanted to give Huck a home under her roof and have him educated. She also said that when she could spare the money, she

---

[1] **astonishment**—complete surprise.

would start him in business. Tom's chance had come. He said: "Huck don't need it. Huck's rich!"

There was a big silence that felt a little awkward to Tom. So he broke it by saying: "Huck's got money. Maybe you don't believe it, but he's got lots of it. I reckon I can show you. You just wait a minute."

Tom ran out of doors. The company looked at each other with interest. They also stared at Huck, who was tongue-tied.

Tom entered the room again, struggling with the weight of his bags. Then he poured the mass of yellow coins upon the table and said—

"There! What did I tell you? Half of it's Huck's and half of it's mine!"

The sight of the gold took everyone's breath away. Nobody spoke for a moment. Then everyone shouted for an explanation. Tom said he could give one, and he did. The tale was long, but the group was fascinated. When he finished, the money was counted. The sum amounted to a little over twelve thousand dollars. It was more money than anyone present had ever seen at one time before.

CHAPTER THIRTY-THREE

Respectable Huck Joins the Gang

Tom and Huck are now respected and admired. Huck is uncomfortable in that role and threatens to run away.

The reader may rest satisfied that Tom's and Huck's **windfall**[1] made a mighty stir in the poor little village of St. Petersburg. So huge a sum, all in actual cash, seemed just about incredible. Wherever Tom and Huck appeared, they were praised, admired, and stared at. Although the boys used to be ignored by the adults, everything they said now was treasured and repeated.

The Widow Douglas lent Huck's money out at six percent interest. Judge Thatcher did the same

---

[1] **windfall**—unexpected gain of money.

with Tom's, at Polly's request. Each lad had an income, now, that was simply huge: a dollar for every weekday in the year and half of the Sundays. Huck and Tom were very, very wealthy.

Thanks to his newfound wealth and the Widow Douglas's protection, Huck Finn found himself dragged into society, where he suffered more than he could bear. The Widow's servants kept him clean and neat and combed and brushed. He had to eat with knife and fork, and he had to use a napkin, cup, and plate. He had to study his schoolbooks, go to church, and talk properly. Wherever he turned, the bars and **shackles**[2] of civilization shut him in and tied him up hand and foot.

He bravely lived with this misery for three weeks, and then one day he turned up missing. For forty-eight hours, the Widow hunted for him everywhere. She was terribly worried, and so was the rest of the town. They searched high and low, and dragged the river for his body. Early the third morning, Tom Sawyer wisely went poking among some empty barrels behind the old slaughter-house. In one of them he found Huck.

Huck had been sleeping there for a couple of days. He had just breakfasted on some stolen odds

---

[2] **shackles**—chains.

and ends of food and was lying now, completely happy, smoking his pipe. He was unkempt, uncombed, and dressed in some of the old rags that he used to wear. Tom told him the trouble he had been causing and urged him to go home. Huck's face lost its happy expression. He said:

"Don't talk about it, Tom. I've tried it, and it don't work."

"Don't talk about it, Tom. I've tried it, and it don't work. It don't work, Tom. The Widow's good to me, and friendly, but I can't stand all those rules. She makes me git up just at the same time every morning. She makes me wash, and then they comb me all to thunder. She won't let me sleep in the wood-shed. I got to wear those awful clothes that just smother me, Tom, and they're so rotten nice that I can't sit down. I got to go to church and sweat and sweat. The Widow eats by a bell, she goes to bed by a bell, and she gets up by a bell. Everything's so awful reg'lar a body can't stand it."

"Well, everybody lives that way, Huck."

"Looky here, Tom, being rich ain't what it's cracked up to be. It's just worry and worry, and sweat and sweat, and a-wishing you was dead all the time. Now these clothes suits me, and this barrel suits me, and I ain't ever going back. Tom, I want you to take my money. I don' want it anymore. It's not doin' me a bit of good. And will you go tell the Widow that I can't come back?"

"Oh, Huck, you know I can't do that. It ain't fair. Besides, if you'll try this thing just a while longer, you'll come to like it."

"Like it! Yes—the way I'd like a hot stove if I was to set on it long enough. No, Tom, I don't want to be rich and I don't want to live in them awful smothery houses anymore. I like the woods, and the river, and the barrels, and I'll stick with them. Besides, what about all that talk about bein' a robber?"

Tom saw his opportunity. "Looky-here, Huck, being rich ain't going to keep me from turning robber."

"No! Oh, good-licks, are you tellin' me the truth, Tom?"

"You know I am. I ain't lying, Huck. But we can't let you into the gang if you ain't respectable, you know."

Huck's disappointment was terrible. "Can't let me in, Tom? Didn't you let me go for a pirate?"

"Yes, but that's different. A robber is more respectable than a pirate. In most countries they're awful high up in the nobility. They're dukes and such."

"Now Tom, ain't you always been friendly to me? You wouldn't shut me out, would you, Tom? You wouldn't do that, now, would you, Tom?"

"Huck, I wouldn't want to, and I don't want to—but what would people say? Why they'd say, 'Mph! Tom Sawyer's Gang! Pretty low characters in it!' They'd mean you, Huck. You wouldn't like that, and I wouldn't either."

Huck was silent for some time, busy with a mental struggle. Finally he said: "Well, I'll go back to the Widow for a month and see if I can stand it, if you'll let me join the gang, Tom."

"All right, Huck, it's a deal! Come along, old chap, and I'll ask the Widow to let up on you a little, Huck."

"Will you Tom—now will you? That's good. If she'll let up on some of the roughest things, I might be able to stand it. When you going to start the gang and turn robbers?"

"Oh, right off. We'll get the boys together and have the initiation tonight, maybe."

"Have the which?"

"Have the initiation."

"What's that?"

"It means you swear to stand by one another, and never tell the gang's secrets, even if you're chopped all to pieces, and kill anybody and all his family that hurts one of the gang."

"That's gay—that's mighty gay, Tom, I tell you."

"Well, I bet it is. And the initiation's got to be done at midnight, in the lonesomest, awfulest place you can find. A haunted house is the best, but they're all ripped up now."

"Well, midnight's good, anyway, Tom."

"Yes, so it is. And you've got to swear on a coffin, and sign it with blood."

"Now that's something great! Why, it's a million times better than pirating. I'll stick with the Widow until I rot, Tom. And if I git to be a really great robber, and everybody starts talkin' about it, I reckon she'll be proud that she took me up an' raised me to be respectable."

THE END